Praise for *BELIEVE*

There is a difference between saying we believe and knowing we believe. Dr. Van has written a book that will help us to truly know what we've been saying all along. Read. Receive. *BELIEVE!*

~Tim Ross
Upset The World
B-Side

I've known Dr. Van Moody for decades and one thing that remains a constant is his primary calling to help people. In his latest book *BELIEVE*, he continues helping. Helping us understand we need to Believe and why understanding and applying that is critical to our Christian life. You'll want to share this book with all believers who want to grow.

~ Sam Chand
Leadership Consultant and Author

BELIEVE: Discover Real Biblical Faith and Why It Matters So Much by Van Moody is an essential read for anyone seeking to deepen their understanding of faith. Dr. Moody masterfully articulates the critical role of faith in navigating life's challenges and enhancing one's relationship with God. This book not only explores the biblical foundation of faith but also provides practical guidance for living a life anchored in deep belief and trust in God's promises. This volume is a wonderful resource for individuals and churches desiring a deeper faith, a more committed relationship with the Lord, and increased fidelity to scripture.

~ Rev. Dr. Stephen Chapin Garner
The Congregational Church of New Canaan

Dr. Van Moody has written a must-read for the times in which we live. As we look around, we find people falling to pieces, because they have lost hope. People have been putting their faith in external measures only to receive disappointment in return. In the midst of watching tv news, and social media news, we cannot forget about the Good News. His real-life examples aligned with Biblical principles will speak to Christians and non-Christians alike. So much is going on in the world and Believe serves to sooth our souls and remind us that God fueled faith leads us to the more excellent way. This insightful, impactful book is filled with instruction for those that need to find faith and redirection for those needing to rekindle their faith. This book builds a house for our faith and provides tools needed to insure it is built on a firm foundation. I found myself hanging on to every word of *BELIEVE*! This is the book I wish I had during a critical, crisis filled juncture in my life. My faith was on the fringes and at risk of slipping away. It is my sincere prayer that this book makes its way to the hands of many that need to be comforted, convicted, challenged, and compelled to be better because they *believe*.

~Tamieka Nicole Gerow
Pastor, Leadership Coach and Facilitator

Whether one is a seasoned believer or someone exploring matters of faith for the first time, Dr. Van Moody's new book provides invaluable clarity and perspective. It is evident that the goal of this book is not merely to impart knowledge but to inspire genuine transformation in the lives of those who read it. *BELIEVE* is a remarkable testament to Dr. Van Moody's deep insight, unwavering faith, and passion for sharing the timeless truths of Scripture with others.

In his latest work *BELIEVE*, Dr. Van Moody reveals faith not only as the foundational building block of a well-formed spirituality, but the very means by which the invisible God manifests His unseen will into the visible world (through us). *BELIEVE* is an invitation to those who seek to reignite their faith and a guide for all who refuse to live beneath their divine potential.

~ *Wayne Chaney*
Influencer, TV Personality, Sr Pastor
Antioch Church of Long Beach

I confess a sense of fear in the face of this invitation into the topic of faith. My fear is that many will pass up this work due to the grip of their assumed familiarity. Dr. Moody accurately points out the abused, misused, and misunderstood concepts of faith. However, by faith I trust that your steps have been providentially prepared, ordered and poised for this journey; that you did not pick it up by accident. Prepare for a journey of and into faith. I assure you this is not an exhibition of theologizing or philosophizing but Dr. Moody practicalizes theory and humanizes the divine principle of faith. This is not a high shelf offering of lofty pseudo-deep arguments of a hackneyed, frequently tossed around, spiritual catch phrase. This is not a sermon. It is not a Sunday school lesson. It is a revelation of a mandatory contemporary mindset for victory, success, and productivity in the both the natural and spiritual realm. Be blessed as you grow in faith!

~*Bishop Kenneth C. Ulmer*
Presiding Bishop:
Macedonia International Bible Fellowship

I have no doubt that it will continue to touch the hearts and minds of countless individuals seeking to deepen their understanding of faith.

~*Matthew Hester, ThD*
Author, Pastor: Dominion Church International

In an era where the Biblical illiteracy gap seems to be growing wider and wider, Dr. Van Moody's book, *BELIEVE*, is a must-read! *BELIEVE* takes the reader on a compelling journey of true faith and its necessity. In essence, faith is the essential ingredient in the life of every believer, and Dr. Moody does an incredible job articulating faith lived out. Contrary to misguided faith ideologies such as "name it and claim it, blab it and grab it," Dr. Moody communicates a faith deeply rooted in Scripture. His ability to teach theologically and practically is par excellence. This book will transform your life if you are serious about growing your faith.

~*Dr. John-Paul C. Foster*
Senior Pastor, Faithful Central Bible Church
Adjunct Professor, Biola University, Talbot School of Theology

BELIEVE

Discover Real Biblical Faith
And Why It Matters So Much

VAN MOODY

Cover design by LaMonte Austin
Author photo on cover by Andrew van Tilborgh

ISBN: 979-8-218370-81-7

ISBN: 979-8-218370-82-4 (eBook)

Jesus answered, "The work of God is this: to <u>believe</u> in the one he has sent."
John 6:29 (NIV)

DEDICATION

To Ty: Thank you for supporting my every step of faith.

To Eden & Ethan: Trust God and He will do more in your life than you ever imagined. I am a witness!

To The Worship Center Family: In order to please God, we have to Believe God. Keep Believing!

CONTENTS

Introduction

One of the reasons real Biblical faith is so critically
important is because many in our country and around
the world are choosing to no longer believe in God.
Many have lost confidence in the political, social,
economic, and religious systems of their nations
and opted out of mainstream life. Many no longer
think there can be peace on earth or that the United
Nations can prevent wars. Others have given up on
politicians' efforts to solve our national problems and
the ability of scientists to meet our growing medical and
environmental challenges. Still others live in daily fear
of terrorism or feel they can only stand by helplessly
and watch the devaluation of human life through ethnic
cleansing, abortion campaigns, and wars.

Humanity has been led to a critical crossroad, left
wondering if there is an alternative to the world as we
have made it. In essence, a lot of people have simply
stopped believing in anything or anyone – they have
simply lost their faith in faith.

While it is absolutely tragic to lose a job, to lose a
spouse, to lose a child, or a home, or a business, these
are not the greatest losses one can experience. The
greatest loss in life on earth is the loss of belief. When
one loses the ability to believe, one loses both faith and
hope! When hope is lost, purpose is cancelled and life is
robbed of meaning.

Introduction

Belief is the raw material required for commitment, persistence, and faithfulness. When belief is lost, life has no explanation. Faith gives us hope, so if faith is lost, hope flees away like mist in the wind. Loss of faith leads to loss of hope, which leads to despair. Life becomes pointless and without value.

The poorest person on earth is the person without faith. No man or woman can live beyond their belief, for without faith all hope is lost. If we believe big, our life is full of endless possibilities, limitless opportunities. If our belief is gone, our life shrinks because possibilities become limited and our expectations are low. It has been the enemy's plan from the very beginning.

If we go back and study what the enemy did to bring about the original sin, we see the evidence of the enemy's plan and how he carried it out. The enemy caused Eve to doubt and no longer believe God. He simply asked, "Did God really say...?" He sowed the seeds of doubt in her heart and mind. It ultimately led her to not believe God. This has been the enemy's plan from the very beginning.

Introduction

The devil is not after our money – he doesn't need it. He's not after our house, our clothes, our spouse, our children, or anything else we think he is after. He is coming for only one thing—our faith. He knows if he can steal our faith so we no longer believe God, everything else in our lives will fall apart. He knows if he can steal our faith, we will be spiritually bankrupt and unable to fulfill the purpose for which God put us on the planet. We will no longer believe God exists or that He responds to us when we seek Him.

This summer my family and I went on sabbatical to Europe for a month. The first two weeks we were in southern Spain, Costa del Sol, Málaga, Marbella, and then we spent a week on the Amalfi Coast of Italy, ending our journey with a week in Paris for our daughter's sixteenth birthday – her dream sweet sixteen. Europe is a beautiful place, the food is delectable, southern Spain in amazing, the Amalfi Coast is breathtaking, Paris is stunning.

But there is one thing I didn't like about Paris – they don't have many available public restrooms and the ones that are available require payment. There were a few times we were in need of a restroom, once while we were at the Louvre waiting to see the Mona Lisa.

Introduction

It was one of those times, the need is great and you call on the Lord because you have to get to the restroom. To get there, you have to pay but they don't accept the dollar, you have to use the euro. Another instance, a beautiful day on the Avenue des Champs-Élysées, I again found myself in search of a restroom. I went into a store and asked, and was told "no." I finally found a restroom and the line was around the corner. Again, I prayed and finally made it to the door. No pennies, dimes, nickels, or quarters accepted, only a euro. I'm grateful I had the right currency this time so I could stop dancing and praying and get in the door to transact business if you know what I mean!

Why this story? Many of us are dancing around, praying, crying out to the Lord, and trying to transact Kingdom business but we do not have the right currency! Faith is the currency of the Kingdom of God. It is the very reason the Bible talks so much about faith. It is the reason Hebrews 11:6 is so important – *"And without faith it is impossible to please God because anyone who comes to him must believe that he exists and that he rewards those who earnestly seek him."*

Introduction

In fact, it is the key verse for us in this book. If we want to please God, we have to believe God. In order to believe, we have to have faith, real faith, but before we can have it we have to know exactly what it is. Let's begin, first by finding out what real Bible faith is and second by discovering why it is so important.

Chapter 1
What is Faith?

"And without faith it is impossible to please God because anyone who comes to him must believe that he exists and that he rewards those who earnestly seek him."
~ Hebrews 11:6

In Hebrews 11:6, God's Word tells us, "And without faith it is impossible to please God, because anyone who comes to him must believe that he exists and that he rewards those who earnestly seek him." This verse will serve as our cornerstone in the discovery of real Biblical faith and its significance in our lives.

What Is Faith?

Faith is one of the most abused, misused, and misunderstood concepts in human life. Throughout history faith has been perceived in many different ways, both inside and outside of religious circles. In the name of faith, people have raped, pillaged, plundered, oppressed, and murdered on a massive scale.

BELIEVE

Over the past century, more people have been killed for their faith or in the name of faith than in every preceding century of human history combined. In many cases, those doing the killing have done so with the firm belief that they were serving God. Even within the Christian Church, faith has been abused and misappropriated for selfish gain so often, now even the Church is attacked and held in contempt by those who don't truly understand it.

What, then, is faith? How do we define it biblically and truthfully, away from all of the misinterpretations, misunderstandings, and misuses?

In Hebrews 11:1, God's Word tells us, *"Now faith is being sure of what we hope for and certain of what we do not see."* The Greek word translated as "faith" here (and most often in the New Testament) is pistis. Pistis means belief, but more than just acceptance or casual belief.

What Is Faith?

It refers instead to a deeply held belief. Pistis also means persuaded, so someone who has pistis is persuaded at a deep level that something is true. Another way to describe pistis is to understand it as confident expectation.

It is exactly what Hebrews 11:1 describes. Confident expectation is *"being sure of what we hope for and certain of what we do not see."* We cannot have true faith or true pistis and not expect something positive to happen. With pistis we can confidently expect and patiently wait for God to act for our good and His glory, even when we can see no visible evidence of anything happening.

The writer of Hebrews, when he penned the words, and it was translated in the KJV, says, *"Now faith is the substance of things hoped for, the evidence of things not seen."* In this translation, chapter 11 verse 1 clearly defines faith in three words – faith, substance, evidence.

We already defined the meaning of the word "faith" so now we will explore the original Greek and the meaning of "substance" and "evidence".

BELIEVE

The word in the Greek translated as "substance" is *hypostasis* and it literally means "to stand under and to support." Faith is to the believer what a foundation is to a house. The first thing builders do is lay the foundation and then test it to make sure it is strong enough to support the house or building to be constructed upon it. Faith is the substance – to stand under to support – the substance is the confidence and assurance we are standing on and building upon.

How are we standing on the substance? It is the result of the third word, evidence. The word translated as "evidence", *elenchus*, literally means an inward conviction from God that what He has promised, He will perform. It is the internal conviction we have that God will keep His Word.

Let's put it all together: *"Faith (**pistis**) is the substance (**hypostasis**) of things hoped for, the evidence (**elenchus**) of things not seen."* Faith (pistis) is a deeply held belief and confident expectation. How do we know?

What Is Faith?

The substance (*hypostasis*) is the firm foundation on which we are building and standing. How do we know we are on a firm foundation?

We have the evidence (*elenchus*), the inward conviction from God that He will keep His Word, what He promised, He will perform!

To be clear – this is not the same as worldly hope. Worldly hope is something we hope for but we have no certainty we will receive it. It is "I hope I get this job" or "I hope I get this promotion" but there is no certainty that we will.

Biblical faith, real faith, is not an "I hope so." Biblical faith is certain because it is anchored on the integrity and promises of the Word of God. Again, the author of Hebrews elaborates in Hebrews 6:19a, *"We have this hope as an anchor for the soul, firm and secure."*

BELIEVE

When we read the list of those who exemplified real Biblical faith in Hebrews 11, we have to acknowledge people often laughed at them because it seemed that what they did made no sense. Abraham left everything he knew and didn't even know where he was going – it made no sense to those around him. How was he able to do that? He had pistis (faith), a deeply held belief, a confident expectation. He had substance (*hypostasis*), he was standing and building on a firm foundation – God's Word. He had evidence (*elenchus*), the firmly held conviction that God, who gave him the Word, was going to do what He said He would do in His Word.

We know, when Noah began building the ark because God told Him it was going to rain – though it had never rained before – people thought he was crazy. They thought he had too much wine and they laughed at him, but he kept building. Why? He had pistis (faith), a deeply held belief, a confident expectation. He had substance (*hypostasis*), he was building the boat on a firm foundation. He had evidence (*elenchus*), the firmly held conviction that God was going to keep His Word – the rain was coming.

What Is Faith?

They all carried on, knowing the One in whom they put their faith and hope. Real Biblical faith drives action as James testifies in James 2:26b, "...*faith without works is dead.*" Genuine Biblical faith produces actions and results in good works – not the other way around. We can do great works and still not have faith but we cannot have faith without faith producing action and good works in our lives.

For example in Matthew 9:27-30a, Matthew writes, "*As Jesus went on from there, two blind men followed him, calling out, 'Have mercy on us, Son of David!' When he had gone indoors, the blind men came to him, and he asked them, 'Do you believe that I am able to do this?' 'Yes, Lord,' they replied. Then he touched their eyes and said, 'According to your faith let it be done to you'; and their sight was restored.*"

Biblical faith is not only practical but very straightforward. These two blind men came after Jesus calling out for healing, but take note, Jesus didn't ask them how many prayers they had prayed or how much money they had. Rather, He asked one simple question, "Do you believe I am able to do this?"

BELIEVE

Translation, "Do you have the right currency for this transaction?" Faith is the currency needed to transact business in the Kingdom of God. They had pistis (faith), a deeply held belief, a confident expectation – they believed all they needed to do was get to Jesus in order to be healed. They had substance (hypostasis), a firm foundation. They had evidence (elenchus), a firmly held conviction. They called Jesus "Son of David" a title that comes from the promise God made to David of a kingdom with no end meaning that even after Solomon there was someone in the Davidic line who was coming with a kingdom that had no end. They knew God promised David's descendants would have a kingdom that had no end. They knew who Jesus truly was – Son of David, Lord, King – Lord over their blindness, their ailments, their illnesses. They knew Jesus was the manifestation of the promise and He could heal them. These guys had it all – pistis (faith), hypostasis (substance), and elenchus (evidence) – and they knew God would do exactly what He said He would do and it was exactly what they needed to be healed.

What Is Faith?

Faith in What?

We exercise faith on a daily basis in any number of objects. One of the most common is the chair. When we sit down in a chair, we don't stop to inspect it, worried it might collapse. We have faith that the chair will hold us.

It's not a matter of how much faith we have, but it is a matter of where your faith is placed. We exercise faith when we sit down on any chair. We exercise faith every time we get behind the wheel of a car, get on a plane, leave the house in the morning, or drop our kids off at school. We exercise faith daily, in lots of ways, but the issue for so many people is that their faith is in the wrong place.

The sixth chapter of John's Gospel opens with the miraculous account of Jesus feeding a crowd of 5,000 people with only five loaves of bread and two fish. Afterward, He retreated into the hills to be alone while His disciples sailed their boat to the other side of the sea of Galilee.

BELIEVE

Later that night, He joined them in the boat by walking to them on the water. The next day, the crowd who had been fed so miraculously the day before went looking for Jesus but could not find Him. The story continues in John 6:24-27:

> Once the crowd realized that neither Jesus nor his disciples were there, they got into the boats and went to Capernaum in search of Jesus. When they found him on the other side of the lake, they asked him, 'Rabbi, when did you get here?'
>
> Jesus answered, 'Very truly I tell you, you are looking for me, not because you saw the signs I performed but because you ate the loaves and had your fill. Do not work for food that spoils, but for food that endures to eternal life, which the Son of Man will give you. For on him God the Father has placed his seal of approval.'

What Is Faith?

In essence, Jesus says, "I know why y'all are looking for me, you want more bread and fish…"

Like all of us, I love the blessings of God as much as anyone, but that is not the point. The point is we should not put our faith in things that can go away. Instead, we should place our trust in Christ. The only thing in life that is sealed and secured is Christ. He is the only trustworthy and reliable object of our faith – not His blessings, not His provisions, not His healings, but only in Jesus Christ Himself.

Where is your faith? Is it in God or is it in what He can do for you?

The example of the chair is so significant because often we place our faith in the wrong places – in people, in money, in education, or in other things God has done. The point Jesus is making in John 6 is our faith should be in Him. Real biblical faith is in God and what He has said, not what He has done.

BELIEVE

John continues the story in John 6:28-33:

> *Then they asked him, 'What must we do to do the works God requires?' Jesus answered, 'The work of God is this: to believe in the one he has sent.'*
>
> *So they asked him, 'What sign then will you give that we may see it and believe you? What will you do? Our ancestors ate the manna in the wilderness; as it is written: 'He gave them bread from heaven to eat.'*
> *Jesus said to them, 'Very truly I tell you, it is not Moses who has given you the bread from heaven, but it is my Father who gives you the true bread from heaven. For the bread of God is the bread that comes down from heaven and gives life to the world.'*

The people are truly confused by the depth of what Jesus is saying and ask, "Well if we are not supposed to follow you for the bread and fish then what are we supposed to do?"

What Is Faith?

Jesus responds to them, "Believe in the One the Father sent…" He told them, "You were coming for the bread and the fish, but you should have been coming for Me." In other words, don't believe in the bread and the fish, don't believe in the miracles, but put your faith in the God of the miracles.

This isn't to imply that God is unfaithful or untrustworthy, it means we don't know how God will do what He has promised but we have to trust Him, not His works of the past, to get the job done, the prayer answered, and His will carried out. He may not move this time in the way we expected or in the way He did before, but He will still carry out His Word and His Will.

The source is always more important than the resource. The manufacturer is always more important than the product. The resources change but the source remains. The products change but the manufacturer remains. We shouldn't put our faith in the resources, our faith should be in the Source.

BELIEVE

In John 6:34-35, John continues, *"'Sir,' they said, 'always give us this bread.' Then Jesus declared, 'I am the bread of life. Whoever comes to me will never go hungry, and whoever believes in me will never be thirsty.'"*

Later in the passage, Jesus elucidates on His meaning while teaching in the synagogue in Capernaum, saying, *"'This is the bread that came down from heaven. Your ancestors ate manna and died, but whoever feeds on this bread will live forever.' On hearing it, many of his disciples said, 'This is a hard teaching. Who can accept it?'"*

There was much grumbling and going forward many of His disciples turned away and ceased to follow him. The truth is we don't really know how many disciples Jesus originally had, all we know are the ones who stayed. The majority of the disciples wanted more bread and fish, but then Jesus told them, "Don't put your faith in the bread and the fish, put your faith in Me."

They said, "This is a hard teaching…" and then they left. The Bible says, "many turned back and no longer followed Him."

What Is Faith?

He then turned to the twelve and asked, " *'You do not want to leave too, do you?' Simon Peter answered him, 'Lord, to whom shall we go? You have the words of eternal life. We have come to believe and to know that you are the Holy One of God'"* (John 6:58-60,66-69).

Peter and the twelve got it right. They recognized it was not about trusting the leftover bread and fish, but about trusting Jesus. They put their faith in Him.

Part of the reason we are in the state we are in today is there are far too many "fish and bread" believers trusting the resources rather than the Source. They are following Jesus for the resource and not the Source. The moment the resource is different, not what we wanted or expected, that's when we say, "Oh, I tried church…" or "I tried Jesus." The truth behind those statements is that He tried us and we came up short.

Instead we need to be true believers who trust in the Source, like Shadrach, Meshach, and Abednego, who when faced with the threat of the fiery furnace, replied:

BELIEVE

King Nebuchadnezzar, we do not need to defend ourselves before you in this matter. If we are thrown into the blazing furnace, the God we serve is able to deliver us from it, and he will deliver us from Your Majesty's hand. But even if he does not, we want you to know, Your Majesty, that we will not serve your gods or worship the image of gold you have set up (Daniel 3:16-18).

Shadrach, Meshach, and Abednego said, "We don't know how He will do it, we just know He is able to do it. Maybe He will get us out, maybe He won't but He is still God and we are still going to trust Him." That is real, genuine Biblical faith. We don't know how He will deliver, only that He will. He may do it through a person, or some other way. We don't know how but we do know Who and we know He will – that is real Biblical faith! His ways are not our ways, His thoughts are not our thoughts, He does exceedingly and abundantly above all we are able to ask, think, and imagine. Maybe He closed the door of what was good to open the door of His best for us! We have to place our faith in the right place – the Source not the resource.

What Is Faith?

The Fight of Faith

As most of us have realized, there is a fight going on between faith and fear. In fact, this tremendous battle between fear and faith is the only fight we really have in life. The enemy and the world operate through fear. God operates through faith. The true fight of our lives is between faith and fear. It is the reason the Apostle Paul encourages Timothy, his son in the faith, saying, *"Fight the good fight of the faith..."* (1 Timothy 6:12a). We are all in the same fight, just like Timothy and Paul, a fight of faith versus fear.

Paul practiced what he preached throughout his life as a believer. At the end of his life, his testimony to Timothy was, *"I have fought the good fight, I have finished the race, I have kept the faith"* (2 Timothy 4:7). Paul says, "I was in the fight between faith and fear, and I kept the faith."

Further, Paul explained the concept to his fellow believers in Corinth:
> *For though we live in the world, we do not wage war as the world does.*

BELIEVE

The weapons we fight with are not the weapons of the world. On the contrary, they have divine power to demolish strongholds. We demolish arguments and every pretension that sets itself up against the knowledge of God, and we take captive every thought to make it obedient to Christ (2 Corinthians 10:3-5).

The enemy will use the trials of life – sickness, job challenges, financial difficulties, family drama, and so much more to instill fear and doubt in our hearts with the purpose of causing us to lose hope and stop believing God. That's where the real fight we are in is! It is exactly what the Word describes as the "flaming darts" of the enemy.

The enemy also uses all the challenging things of this world – the news, social media, the words of others, unexpected situations - to cause us to lose hope and stop believing God. That's where the true fight is!

What Is Faith?

In those moments of heartbreak, bad news, despair, and doubt, we have to remember we are in the fight of faith versus fear. The battle remains the same – are we going to let fear control us and fill us with so much doubt that we don't believe God or are we going to push fear away and grab that negative fearful thought and push it out of our minds and still believe God? Are we going to allow our lives to be driven, dictated, and determined by fear or by faith?

God's Word is filled with example after example of genuine fights of faith. In fact, it happened to Jesus quite often. One example is found in Mark 5:21-43. A Jewish leader named Jairus came to Jesus and asked Him to come to his house and heal his daughter who was very sick. As Jesus made His way to Jarius' home, he was distracted by a woman with an issue of blood. She believed, *"If I just touch his clothes, I will be healed."* She touched the hem of Jesus's cloak and was immediately healed.

Jesus knew what had happened in an instant and began to look for the person who had touched Him.

BELIEVE

The disciples answered His query, explaining the crowd was pressing, but Jesus did not give up His search. Finally the woman came forward and confessed the truth – twelve years of her testimony.

Jesus replied, "*Daughter, your faith has healed you. Go in peace and be freed from your suffering.*"

Of course, that wasn't the end of the story, after all Jesus was still needed at the house of Jarius:

> *While Jesus was still speaking, some people came from the house of Jairus, the synagogue leader. 'Your daughter is dead,' they said. 'Why bother the teacher anymore?'*
> *Overhearing what they said,* **Jesus told him, 'Don't be afraid; just believe.'**
>
> *He did not let anyone follow him except Peter, James, and John, the brother of James. When they came to the home of the synagogue leader, Jesus saw a commotion, with people crying and wailing loudly.*

What Is Faith?

He went in and said to them, 'Why all this commotion and wailing? The child is not dead but asleep.' But they laughed at him.

After he put them all out, he took the child's father and mother and the disciples who were with him, and went in where the child was. He took her by the hand and said to her, 'Talitha koum!' (which means 'Little girl, I say to you, get up!').

Immediately the girl stood up and began to walk around (she was twelve years old). At this, they were completely astonished.

The woman fought the crowd to reach Jesus, believing all she need do was touch His garment and be healed. She had faith in the Source and overcame her fear.

Jarius was in a fight. He fought doubt brought on by what the world was saying and believed Jesus instead. He had faith in the Source and overcame his fears.

BELIEVE

We are all in the fight – fear versus faith. What will you do when unexpected news comes and fear threatens your faith? We are in a fight and we need to choose faith!

In Romans 4:18-24, we see the fight of faith against fear in the life of Abraham:

> *Against all hope, Abraham in hope believed and so became the father of many nations, just as it had been said to him, 'So shall your offspring be.' Without weakening in his faith, he faced the fact that his body was as good as dead—since he was about a hundred years old—and that Sarah's womb was also dead. Yet he did not waver through unbelief regarding the promise of God, but was strengthened in his faith and gave glory to God, being fully persuaded that God had power to do what he had promised. . This is why 'it was credited to him as righteousness.' The words 'it was credited to him' were written not for him alone, but also for us, to whom God will credit righteousness—for us who believe in him who raised Jesus our Lord from the dead.*

What Is Faith?

Abraham did not ignore the fact that he had no children, but rather he chose to believe God and have faith. He did not ignore the fact that his body was "as good as dead" but chose faith in God's Word. Abraham had faith that God had the power to do what He promised.

Abraham had *pistis* (faith), *hypostasis* (substance), and *elenchus* (evidence). He knew God would be true to His Word.

Our fight of faith against fear and unbelief begins and ends with the Source – God who has the power to do what He promises, just as He did for Abraham. "It was credited to him as righteousness" but those words are not written just for Abraham for God will "credit righteousness" for all of us who believe in Him who raised Jesus from the dead.

Choose faith. Trust God. Believe.

BELIEVE

Reflection

Where do you feel your faith is in this moment - on a scale of 1 to 10? Why?

Can you think of a time when you felt your faith was lost or incredibly low? What did you do to regain your faith?

Where is your faith? Is it in God or is it in what He can do for you?

Like those we read about in John 6, have you considered leaving Him too? When have you trusted the bread and fish, but not Jesus? How can you turn from trusting the bread and the fish to trusting the One who provides it all?

What will you do when unexpected news comes and fear threatens your faith? Pray right now to overcome fear in the fight of faith.

Chapter 2
Why Is Faith So Important?

"For indeed the gospel was preached to us as well as to them; but the word which they heard did not profit them, not being mixed with faith in those who heard it."
~ Hebrews 4:2

As we begin this chapter, it is important to note that the writer of Hebrews, for much of the book, offers a commentary on the Old Testament/Old Covenant in order for us as readers to understand the New Testament/New Covenant reality that we have with God through Jesus Christ.

In Hebrews 4:2, he writes, *"For indeed the gospel was preached to us as well as to them; but the word which they heard did not profit them, not being mixed with faith in those who heard it."* The nation of Israel heard the Word. God spoke to them in a variety of ways, but the Word did not benefit them because they did not combine it with faith.

It is a profound statement, one which we should all heed. They heard the Word of God, loud and clear and powerful, but they did not believe.

BELIEVE

In January of 2019, the weekend of Martin Luther King, Jr.'s holiday, my wife and I got word that my mother was not doing well. She was complaining of stomach and back pains. My stepfather took her to the hospital on Saturday. On Sunday, my wife and I decided we needed to go over to Atlanta and check on my mom. We were in Birmingham and after our services, we got in the car and drove to see my mother in the hospital there.

We got there to find her complaining of severe back and stomach pain. Doctors came in and out on Sunday. They took her for a variety of tests but they couldn't find anything. They were uncertain of what was going on but determined. They decided to keep her overnight and call in specialists on Monday morning to do some more specialized testing. They explained, "As far as we can tell, we have not detected any kind of issue but we believe the pain you are experiencing is real."

My wife and I booked a room in the hotel just around the corner from the hospital for the night. In the morning, on the holiday, we returned to the hospital and the specialists were already there.

Why Is Faith So Important?

They did a battery of tests that day. When they returned, they said, "We think we have identified the issue. We believe you have pancreatic cancer. Unfortunately it is Stage 4."

We immediately responded, "What does this mean? What do we need to do?" The doctors answered, "There is really not much we can do because of the advanced stage of the cancer."

My mother had successfully gone through two bouts with breast cancer, believing God as we stood together as a family. She had gone through it well and the doctors felt confident they had gotten all of the cancer.

But when the doctors came into the room and said, "You have Stage 4 pancreatic cancer," my mother's countenance fell and she basically shut down.

The last conversation I had with my mother was when the doctors left the room and I leaned over, hugged, and kissed her, and encouraged her, "Mom, God can bring us through this. We can get through this with God."

BELIEVE

She agreed, "Okay," but she said it in a way in which it was clear she was giving up.

It was the last communication I would have with my mother. They gave her two weeks but my mother lasted just over four weeks. She never spoke again. It was not because of the medication, nor how extensive the pain was, she simply chose not to say a word because she had given up.

My mother passed away and it was a difficult loss for my sister and I and our family, but God has given us the grace to get through it.

Several months after my mother's passing an Elder in our church, came to me and said, "Hey, I met a woman, a phenomenal African American entrepreneur who is doing incredible things down in Mobile, AL and I think you should meet her."

She continued, "If you are open, she will be in town and would love to have lunch with you." She also shared with me that this woman was also a friend of John Grey's mother.

Why Is Faith So Important?

I knew John Grey well as he has spoken at our church a number of times.

I agreed to the meeting and she set up the opportunity for me to go to lunch with this woman. It just so happened that on that day, the woman was to also be with John Grey's mom. I went to the restaurant where I was to meet the woman from Mobile. She was running late, but John Grey's mother had already arrived. She greeted me and we sat down in a booth. We were talking, and she asked about me and my background and the ministry. I told her and then she said, "Well, tell me about your parents."

I answered, "My dad is still with us, but we just lost my mother."

She offered, "Oh I am so sorry. Tell me about her."

I continued, "My mom passed from Stage 4 pancreatic cancer a few months ago."

She said, "Really?" I nodded and she paused, "Do you mind if I tell you a story?"

BELIEVE

I said, "No," after all I was really there waiting on the woman from Mobile.

She began, "A few years ago I was diagnosed with Stage 4 pancreatic cancer. The doctors only gave me a few weeks to live but then you know, I got really excited."

I asked, "You got excited?" She replied, "Yes, when I got the diagnosis, I got excited because I knew it was an opportunity for God to show up."

I was confused but responded "Okay," and she continued her story. "I went through the scriptures and I found every verse that spoke to God's ability to heal me. Every day I read those scriptures, every day I confessed those scriptures over my life. My family rallied around me but I wouldn't allow my family members who didn't have faith to be around me. All my family who believed God and confessed the Word rallied around me and spoke those Words over my life.

Why Is Faith So Important?

When I went back to the doctor, I told him, 'I am healed'.
The doctors thought I was crazy but then I lived beyond
those few months they had given me to live. The doctors
didn't understand it so they said they needed to test
me again. And do you know what, when they tested me
again, they couldn't find the cancer."

She was telling me all this and on the outside I was
responding, "Oh praise the Lord," but on the inside I was
falling apart. What was difficult for me to wrap my mind
around was the stark contrast between my mother's
outcome and this woman's outcome.

Later, I did meet the woman from Mobile, an incredible
woman of faith, and multi-millionaire. When she arrived
at the restaurant she told me the story of how God
grew her business enterprises and made her a multi-
millionaire. I sat and listened to her story and I even
responded, "Oh that's really incredible," but on the inside
I wasn't really paying attention to her story because I
was so blown away by what John Grey's mother had told
me earlier about her healing from Stage 4 pancreatic
cancer – the same diagnosis that my mother died from.

BELIEVE

After my lunch meeting with the woman from Mobile ended, I left the restaurant, got in my car, and wept. Why was the outcome for John Grey's mom different than the outcome for my mother? My mother knew the Lord, she grew up in the church, and after retiring from corporate America, she went to seminary, got a degree in theology, and pastored two churches in Atlanta. My mother knew the Word, my mother preached the Word, but when she got that diagnosis, she didn't believe the Word.

The writer of Hebrews in chapter four says the nation of Israel heard the same Word we heard but it didn't benefit them because they didn't believe. They did not mix with faith the Word they had heard.

The difference between my mother's outcome and John Grey's mother's outcome – same diagnosis – was that my mom, out of fear, anxiety, and worry, didn't believe and she shut down. John Grey's mom got excited and stood on the Word of God. She believed and she mixed it with faith and she is still here today!

Why Is Faith So Important?

The realization was heavy for me and I spent much of 2019 grieving over my mother's loss but even in my grief, God was speaking to me.

Maybe you find yourself in a similar situation, maybe you are at a crossroad yourself, but wherever you are and whatever you are facing, if you can hear the Word and mix it with faith, God can make things happen, God can change things!

Faith Activates God's Promises

The promises of God are not automatic. They have to be appropriated (we have to make them ours) and activate them by faith. In the last chapter we learned that real, Biblical faith results in action - *pistis* (faith), *hypostasis* (substance), and *elenchus* (evidence). *Pistis* is a deeply held belief, a confident expectation. *Hypostasis* is the ground you are standing on and building on – your foundation. *Elenchus* is the evidence – God is going to fulfill His Word.

We need to also understand it in reverse, when we have the evidence, the inward conviction because we have the Word of God, and we believe God is going to fulfill His Word, then we can mix it with faith.

BELIEVE

It means we do something with it. We don't just say we believe, but we build from evidence to substance, speaking and acting from the foundation, which, in turn, activates the promises of God.

The Bible testifies to the power of God's Word and His promises. In Psalm 119:89, we read, *"Forever, O Lord, your word is settled in heaven."* Notice the verse does not say "your Word is established on the earth."

In Isaiah 55:11, God testifies again to the power of His Word, *"So is my word that goes out from my mouth: It will not return to me empty, but will accomplish what I desire and achieve the purpose for which I sent it."* God's Word is powerful, never coming back empty-handed, but always accomplishing the work He intended, completing the assignment He gave.

How then is that manifest on the earth? Paul tells us in 2 Corinthians 13:1, "By the mouth of two or three witnesses every word shall be established." God's Word is clear in this – a matter becomes manifest after two or three witnesses testify.

Why Is Faith So Important?

Believing God's Word is the first step, and speaking and acting on it is step two in activating the promises of God.

Paul offers further testimony in 2 Corinthians 1:20, *"For no matter how many promises God has made, they are "Yes" in Christ. And so through him the "Amen" is spoken by us to the glory of God."* When we believe the Word of God we have taken the first step, but we must continue the next step of faith by speaking the Word of God and acting on the Word of God to set the promises of God in motion knowing He fulfills all of His promises in Christ.

It is settled in heaven but we establish and settle it in earth by speaking and acting on the Word. Our belief is simply the first step of faith needed to activate the power of His Word and His promises.

In January of 2023, a friend sent tickets so that my Executive Pastor and I, along with our sons, could attend the College Football Playoff's National Championship in Los Angeles. He explained all I had to do was open the email and accept what he sent and the four tickets would be on my phone.

BELIEVE

I had the tickets on my phone but didn't know if they would work but we still had to act on what he sent us. We had to get on a plane, fly from Brimingham to L.A., get a hotel, and got to SoFi Stadium with the expectation that these tickets would scan and get us into the game. Had we not acted on his gift, we would not have enjoyed the benefits the gift promised.

The same is true in a much bigger way of all God has promised us, but we must not only believe, we must also act on His Words to activate all He has promised. God has sent us an "email" with "tickets" for our healing, our joy, our victory, our peace, our breakthrough, and so much more but we have to do something with it – show up with the expectation – because the promises of God are not automatic. By faith, we have to activate the promises. We have to believe it, speak it, and act on it and then it is made manifest from heaven to here on earth! It is already settled in heaven but it becomes settled and established on earth when we speak it and act on it.

Why Is Faith So Important?

In Genesis 12, God calls Abraham to "leave your country, your people and your father's household, to the land I will show you." God goes on to tell Abraham, "I will make you into a great nation. You will have a promised son and it is through him that you will go from a father to a family to a nation."

Abraham had his journey of faith and the son of promise, Isaac, is born. The promise of God doesn't stop with Abraham. God says, "through your son the promise will be birthed" – a father to a family to a nation. Abraham tells Isaac God's promises, Isaac gets married to Rebekah but the Bible says Rebekah is barren. So, how is the promise to be fulfilled?

In Genesis 25:21, the writer tells us, *"Now Isaac pleaded with the Lord for his wife, because she was barren; and the Lord granted his plea, and Rebekah his wife conceived."*

Believing the Word of God is the first step, but when we speak the Word and act on the Word, we activate the promises of God and establish them on the earth.

BELIEVE

Isaac's posture wasn't, *"Well if God wants it to happen, it will happen..."* No Isaac said, "God, my daddy told me all the promises You made about me and my wife and our children who would grow into a nation." God had already said it, all that was left was for Isaac to believe it, speak it, and act on the Word which was already established in heaven.

The same is true for us, God has made the promises but we don't establish it in the earth because we don't believe it, speak it, and act on it. Our posture needs to be "Lord You said it...I speak it...I act on it...and establish Your Word on earth." God already said it, it is established in heaven and when we believe it, speak it, and act on it, we establish His Word on the earth. We have to hear the Word and mix it with faith to see it manifest in our lives.

What's most unfortunate is we believe and speak and act on a lot of things that will not help us. We believe the stuff we see on social media, television, and in movies and we share it and act on it, but there is no power in any of that stuff! As believers we have something much more powerful – we have the Word of God, but we have to believe it, speak it, and act on it!

Why Is Faith So Important?

Remember our verse in Hebrews 4:2, *"For indeed the gospel was preached to us as well as to them; but the word which they heard did not profit them, <u>not being mixed with faith in those who heard it</u>."* The nation of Israel wanted to be like everyone else and often we do too, but we are not called to be like the world we are called to follow His all-powerful, eternal Word.

Jesus testifies in Matthew 24:35, *"Heaven and earth will pass away, but my words will never pass away."* The Word of God is eternal and powerful, it will never fail.

The writer of Hebrews tells us, *"The Son is the radiance of God's glory and the exact representation of his being, sustaining all things by his powerful word"* (Hebrews 1:3). The Word of God sustains everything, the sun, the planets, the stars, and more. This is how powerful the Word of God is – holding all things together.

Unbelief is also powerful. We can have access to all of God's promises, but if we don't believe it will not benefit us! We can have access to all of God's promises, but if we fail to believe God's Word, and speak and act on His promises it will NOT benefit us.

BELIEVE

The children of Israel watched Egypt get the ten plagues but none of the plagues hit them. They watched as God made the Egyptians favorably disposed to give them gold, silver, jewels, and more. They experienced God bring them safely out of Egypt. They saw God open the Red Sea for them to walk through and afterward destroy their enemies as he closed the same waters. They ate manna and quail provided by God in the wilderness. Time after time after time they saw the power of God's Word and they still didn't believe. The Word is that powerful, but unbelief is also powerful.

Not one promise from God is empty of power, as the angel sent by God to Mary explained, *"Nothing is impossible with God"* (Luke 1:37). Much like a stick of dynamite, the Word of God has power, but we have to light the fuse. When we believe the Word, speak the Word, and act on the Word, we are lighting the fuse for the Word to come alive and impact our lives by His power.

It may sound difficult to believe but God gave all of that power to us. Genesis 1:26 tells us God created man in His own image and likeness.

Why Is Faith So Important?

Image means nature or character. Mankind was created to be like God in character and nature. We possess the attributes of God.

Mankind was also created in God's likeness. Likeness is not about appearance as much as it is about function. To be created in God's likeness means man was created to function like God. God is a God of faith who functions by faith and we are to do the same.

Whenever we try to function in an environment or manner different from that for which we were created, we end up dysfunctional. In some cases, functioning outside of how God created us to function can even kill us.

For example, if we try to function underwater for very long without some sort of breathing apparatus, we will die. We were not created to live underwater. Fish are designed to live in water; we are not. We were designed to function in an environment of faith, and outside that environment of faith we cannot function properly.

BELIEVE

The absence of faith creates a vacuum which is quickly filled by fear and doubt. In turn, fear and doubt lead to worry and anxiety, which are the antithesis of faith. There is no part of our bodies designed to handle worry.

In fact, scientific research has demonstrated worry activates enzymes which cause our arteries and veins to constrict, thus restricting blood flow, which can then lead to headaches, heart attack, stroke, and other cardiovascular ailments. In other words, if we catch ourselves saying, *"I'm worrying myself to death,"* we are not exaggerating. God created us to function by faith, which means that unless we are functioning by faith, we are self-destructing. Without faith, we kick into worry, anxiety, and mental anguish and depression, which eventually sabotages our lives.

Everything God has for us is accessed by faith including our salvation; our power, deliverance, and healing; and our divine influence, favor, joy, and gifts.

Why Is Faith So Important?

- Our salvation: *But the righteousness that is **by faith** says: "Do not say in your heart, 'Who will ascend into heaven?'" (that is, to bring Christ down) "or 'Who will descend into the deep?'" (that is, to bring Christ up from the dead). But what does it say? "The word is near you; it is in your mouth and in your heart," that is, the message concerning **faith** that we proclaim: If you declare with your mouth, "Jesus is Lord," and believe in your heart that God raised him from the dead, you will be saved. For it is with your heart that you believe and are justified, and it is with your mouth that you profess **your faith** and are saved.* (Romans 10:6-10)

God is not too high or too low but near us. God is not far from us. There is no "saved card" that we can produce to show we are believers. Why? We are saved by faith, believing in our hearts that Jesus is Lord. We not only believed it, we acted on it, confessing with our mouths that Jesus is Lord. We accessed our salvation by faith!

BELIEVE

- Our power, deliverance, and healing: *For I am not ashamed of the gospel, because it is the power of God that brings salvation to everyone **who believes**: first to the Jew, then to the Gentile. For in the gospel the righteousness of God is revealed—a righteousness that is **by faith** from first to last, just as it is written: "The righteous will live **by faith**. (Romans 1:16-17)*

The gospel is the power of God and His power allows us to be exactly who God designed us to be. We can't do our jobs by ourselves, we can't heal ourselves, we can't deliver ourselves, but God can by His power. The word "Salvation" here means more than eternal salvation, it is deliverance, healing, being made completely whole. The power to accomplish any and all of it comes from God not from us and we tap into by faith alone!

- Our divine influence, favor, joy, and gifts: *Through whom we have gained access **by faith** into this grace in which we now stand. And we boast in the hope of the glory of God. (Romans 5:2)*

Why Is Faith So Important?

The word translated as "grace" is *charis* and it means divine influence, favor, joy, gifts of God. It means God will release grace on our lives for the things He has called us to do. God is never concerned about us being adequate but always about us being available. If we say, "Yes, Lord, I am available," God will release His grace on our lives to do what He has called us to do. We tap into that grace by faith because everything God has for us is accessed by faith.

Faith Brings God Pleasure

We often refer to Hebrews 11:6, *"And without faith it is impossible to please God, because anyone who comes to him must believe that he exists and that he rewards those who earnestly seek him."* And yet, sometimes the familiarity of it robs the power that God wants us to truly understand in it.

It does not matter how anointed you are, it does not matter how long you have been saved, it does not matter how many small groups you have lead, it does not matter how many degrees you have – none of it brings God pleasure.

BELIEVE

Without faith, it is impossible to please God! We cannot please God if we are living life (marriage, business, school, parenting, etc.) apart from faith.

On the other hand, if we are living by faith in every aspect of our lives, He promises rewards. He has laid up rewards for us which we can only access through faith. Throughout Scripture, those who grieved God the most were those who had no faith. Conversely, those who pleased God the most were those who lived by faith.

For example, in Mark 6:1-6, Mark tells us:

> *Jesus left there and went to his hometown, accompanied by his disciples. When the Sabbath came, he began to teach in the synagogue, and many who heard him were amazed. 'Where did this man get these things?' ' they asked. 'What's this wisdom that has been given him? What are these remarkable miracles he is performing? Isn't this the carpenter? Isn't this Mary's son and the brother of James, Joseph, Judas, and Simon?*

Why Is Faith So Important?

*Aren't his sisters here with us?' And they took offense at him. Jesus said to them, 'A prophet is not without honor except in his own town, among his relatives and in his own home.' He could not do any miracles there, except lay his hands on a few sick people and heal them. **He was amazed at their lack of faith.***

The people who grieved God the most were the people who had little or no faith. The same is true today.

On the other hand, in Matthew 8:5-13, Matthew explains:

When Jesus had entered Capernaum, a centurion came to him, asking for help. 'Lord,' he said, 'my servant lies at home paralyzed, suffering terribly.' Jesus said to him, 'Shall I come and heal him?' The centurion replied, 'Lord, I do not deserve to have you come under my roof. But just say the word, and my servant will be healed.

BELIEVE

For I myself am a man under authority,
with soldiers under me. I tell this one,
'Go,' and he goes; and that one, 'Come,'
and he comes. I say to my servant,
'Do this,' and he does it.' **When Jesus**
heard this, he was amazed and said to
those following him, 'Truly I tell you,
I have not found anyone in Israel with
such great faith. *I say to you that many*
will come from the east and the west,
and will take their places at the feast
with Abraham, Isaac, and Jacob in the
kingdom of heaven. But the subjects of the
kingdom will be thrown outside, into the
darkness, where there will be weeping and
gnashing of teeth.' Then Jesus said to the
centurion, 'Go! Let it be done just as you
believed it would.' And his servant was
healed at that moment.

We see the same word here – amazed. In the last
passage Jesus was amazed because the people who had
known Him all their lives did not believe Him,

Why Is Faith So Important?

We see the same word here – amazed. In the last passage Jesus was amazed because the people who had known Him all their lives did not believe Him, but this time, He is amazed because the Centurion (a Roman, an outsider to the Jewish faith) has great faith in Him. Jesus was amazed because He had not found anyone in Israel with the same great faith of this man.

In Habakkuk 2:4, God says, *"Behold the proud, His soul is not upright in him; But the just shall live by his faith."* *Do you see the contrast and comparison here? One group of people are proud, their soul is not right in them because they don't have faith. God calls those of us who do not have faith and who do not trust Him proud. Why? We think we can handle life on our own. We think we don't need God, His power, His grace (charis). But God tells us plainly, "the just shall live by faith."*

The writer of Hebrews picks up on this fact in Hebrews 10:38-39, when he writes, *"But **my righteous one will live by faith**. And I take no pleasure in the one who shrinks back. But we do not belong to those who shrink back and are destroyed, **but to those who have faith and are saved**."*

BELIEVE

We know what it means to be those who shrink back. When we get a diagnosis, when we get an email, when life's circumstances don't turn out the way we thought they would and we despair – we shrink back. But God... He reminds us, He has proven Himself to us over and over and over again. He reminds us that we know who He is, how He has helped us in the past, in difficult circumstances. He brings to mind how He has delivered us before and will do it again. He admonishes us not to shrink back because He takes no pleasure in our doubts, our despair, our pride. He reminds us He is the God who makes a way when there is no way. He is the way maker, the miracle worker, the promise keeper God, and He tells us, "Don't shrink back." We are to be the ones who have faith and are saved – the ones who please God.

Paul carries on this theme in his second letter to the Corinthians (2 Corinthians 5:7-9) when he writes, *"For we live by faith, not by sight. We are confident, I say, and would prefer to be away from the body and at home with the Lord. So we **make it our goal to please him**, whether we are at home in the body or away from it."*

Why Is Faith So Important?

We must make it our goal to please Him. The love of God is unconditional. God loves us and there is absolutely nothing we can do about it. He loves us with a love so great, there is nothing we can do to stop His love. Yet, while God's love is unconditional, we are responsible for how pleased he is with us. Like a parent admonishing a child, God will say to us, "I will never stop loving you, but this behavior/decision/action I am not pleased with."

The final question, "Is God pleased with you or are you shrinking back?"

BELIEVE

Reflection

Has there been a time in your life that you heard the Word, but did not believe? Describe it and explain what you learned.

If you are going through a trying time - search the scriptures and note any verses which promise God's help in your situation – read those scriptures daily, speak them over your life, pray them back to God until He answers and then share the outcome.

How can you take the Word of God you have heard and mix it with faith in your current circumstances?

By believing the Word of God, speaking the Word, and acting on the Word, we activate the promises of God and establish them on the earth. Can you give an example of this in your own life?

Is God pleased with you or are you shrinking back?

Chapter 3
Increasing Your Faith

"The apostles said to the Lord,
"Increase our faith!"
~ Luke 17:5

Faith is not just for miracles, it is for everyday life. Even so, most of us, much like the apostles, feel we need to increase our faith, but just how do we grow our faith?

In Romans 12:3, Paul explains, *"For I say, through the grace given to me, to everyone who is among you, not to think of himself more highly than he ought to think, but to think soberly, as God has dealt to each one a measure of faith."* All believers are given a measure of faith and it is our responsibility to steward it. We have three options in doing so – we can grow our faith, neglect our faith, or decrease our faith.

As we already discovered, Jesus, throughout the gospels often speaks of the varying levels of people's faith.

BELIEVE

He mentions those with little faith, great faith, and no faith at all, confirming the truth that there are levels of faith and that it is possible to grow our faith. Paul testifies to this fact in Romans 1:17, where he writes, *"For in it the righteousness of God is revealed **from faith to faith**; as it is written, 'The just shall live by faith.'"*

How Then Do We Increase Our Faith?

Paul, again in his letter to the Romans, tells us in Romans 10:17, the first step we must take to increase our faith, *"So then faith comes by hearing, and hearing by the word of God."* Faith comes by hearing the Word of God. The process of hearing the Word of God begins in our head and then hits our hearts and increases our faith.

If you've ever read a verse in the Bible and all of a sudden thought, *"I can do this! I can do this!"* you've experienced an increase of your faith because you heard the Word of God.

Increasing Your Faith

If you've ever been in a service where a pastor was teaching, and suddenly you realized, *"I can do this! I can do all things through Christ who strengthens me!"* then in that moment you heard the Word of God and your faith increased because of it.

This is the difference between the Bible and self-help books. It's true, self-help books often offer us some good advice, telling us the right things to do to improve ourselves but they do not give us the power to do those things. A self-help book might say, *"If you really want to succeed in life you need to stop worrying."* It's true, really great advice in fact, but that book can't give you the power to stop worrying, because those books aren't backed by the power of God. Their authors aren't imbued with God's power.

The Bible is unlike any other book ever written. It has power, supernatural power within its pages. It has the power to truly change lives, something NO other book has. Why? It has the power to change lives and increase our faith because it is the Word of God. The Word of God is the most powerful entity in the universe.

BELIEVE

In fact, the Bible proclaims the entire universe was created by the Word of God. How? God spoke it into existence.

When Jesus was on earth two thousand plus years ago, He performed profound miracles, even bringing people back to life solely by his Word. His miracles demonstrate the power of God's Word.

I don't have power like that. You don't have power like that because we are not God, but God and His Word are that powerful!

Hebrews 4:12 says it this way, *"The Word of God is living and active, sharper than any double-edged sword, it penetrates even to dividing soul and spirit, joints and marrow; it judges the thoughts and attitudes of the heart."*

The Word of God is actually alive, it is living. The word translated "living" is the Greek word *zoa*. It means to live, living, alive. We get the words "zoo" and "zoology" from it. The Word of God is living (*zoa*). It is alive, not just mere words on a page.

Increasing Your Faith

The Word of God is active. The Greek word *energos* is the word translated here as "active." It means at work, full of energy, effective. It is where we get the word "energy." The Word of God has energy; it has the power to change things effectively.

Unlike self-help books, God's Word not only tells us what to do to improve, but gives us the power to do it as it increases our faith. When we read the thousands of promises in the Bible, we see God telling us if we do "this" then He will do "this" and as a result our expectation and our faith are increased because we know the Word of God is true and living and active.

This is one of the reasons I read through the entire Bible each year and why our S.O.A.P. devotional method is so powerful – it allows us to read, hear, and apply the powerful Word of God daily in our lives year after year and increases our faith.

God's Word warns us in Mark 4:24a, *"And He said to them, 'Be careful what you are hearing...'"*

BELIEVE

The average American spends 53.7 hours per week on screens, and here Jesus tells us, *"Be careful what you hear..."* Why? *Let's keep reading in Mark 4:24b-25, "The measure [of thought and study] you give [to the truth you hear] will be the measure [of virtue and knowledge] that comes back to you..."* In other words, whatever we spend the most time hearing is what our lives will be full of and what is going to come back around in our lives. Therein lies the problem. We are daily encountering problems, issues, difficulties, and challenges for which our "screens" do NOT have the solution. The result, we are faced with challenges and we need answers from the Lord but because 53.7 hours has been spent on our screens we don't receive the direction and answers we desperately need.

Jesus says, "Be careful what you hear..." but he goes on in Mark 4:26-29:

> *And He said, 'The kingdom of God is like*
> *a man who scatters seed upon the ground,*
> *And then continues sleeping and rising*
> *night and day while the seed sprouts and*
> *grows and increases—he knows not how.*

Increasing Your Faith

The earth produces [acting] by itself—
first the blade, then the ear, then the full
grain in the ear. But when the grain is
ripe and permits, immediately he sends
forth [the reapers] and puts in the sickle,
because the harvest stands ready.

Jesus is talking about the Word of God. The Word of God is the seed. Jesus begins by saying, "Be careful what you hear" because if we hear the Word it goes in our heart and our faith will grow over time. As we hear the Word day and night, it takes root in our hearts and begins sprouting up. Faith grows over time. The more we spend time in the scriptures, the more the seed of the Word goes into our hearts and subsequently our faith increases.

But, if we spend 53.7 hours on our screens we aren't hearing the Word as often and, just like our faith can increase, it can also decrease. Increasing our faith requires hearing the Word, but there is more, we also have to heed the Word.

BELIEVE

Heed The Word

In Luke 17, we know the disciples ask, *"Lord, increase our faith."* Jesus responds in Luke 17:6-10:

> *He replied, 'If you have faith as small as a mustard seed, you can say to this mulberry tree, 'Be uprooted and planted in the sea,' and it will obey you. Suppose one of you has a servant plowing or looking after the sheep. Will he say to the servant when he comes in from the field, 'Come along now and sit down to eat'? Won't he rather say, 'Prepare my supper, get yourself ready and wait on me while I eat and drink; after that you may eat and drink'? Will he thank the servant because he did what he was told to do? So you also, when you have done everything you were told to do, should say, 'We are unworthy servants; we have only done our duty.'*

Increasing Your Faith

What in the world is Jesus talking about? They asked Him to help them increase their faith and He begins teaching them about doing their duty. Why? Faith is directly connected to us doing what God has commanded us to do.

There is a connection between our faith growing and our obedience to the Word God gives us. Recently, I had the opportunity to go to Raleigh, North Carolina and speak to a great church. After the service, I had lunch with the leaders.

During our time together, they explained how they wanted to increase their faith, much like the disciples had asked Jesus. They asked me to share how it happened to me, and to our community. I shared with them about the moment I committed to God that I was going to live by faith. In that moment, God gave me a series of important opportunities to be obedient to his Word and the more I was, the more my faith increased. The biggest and scariest opportunity was planting our ministry – The Worship Center.

BELIEVE

The pastor who was responsible for our move from Florida to Birmingham initially shared with me that he believed God called me to plant a church. Having worked as a church consultant for many years, I was acquainted with the challenges of church planting, and I immediately told him I didn't want to be involved with planting a church.

Shortly after I said "no" to him, my wife came to me and shared that the Lord had shown her the same thing – I was to plant a church. I also, very promptly told her that she must have bumped her head and misheard God. She even went as far to tell me that if we had to empty our bank account, sell everything we had, and eat 'pork and beans' from a can, she would be okay with it because she was convinced this was the reason why God brought us to Birmingham.

I promptly told her, "No, I don't want to hear it, and I don't receive that."

A few weeks later, I couldn't sleep one night. It was 3 o'clock in the morning and I could not rest. I got out of the bed, deeply disturbed.

I got up, went to the place in our living room where I always meet with the Lord and pray. As I knelt down and begin to pray, I began to weep, and I couldn't stop. While weeping I told the Lord, "Lord, I don't want to do this."

The Lord began to deal with me, "I thought you said you were going to trust me. I thought you committed to live by faith."

While I continued weeping, my response was, "I know Lord, but I just don't want to do this." I responded this way, only thinking about the financial impact of this type of decision. We would have to empty our savings, drain our 401K, sell our homes, and drastically change our lifestyle.

And then the Lord said to me, as clearly as you are reading these words, "Do you not believe if you give it all to me for this cause that I will give it all back to you?"

I wept and wept and wept out of deep conviction because in that moment I had to admit to God I did not trust Him.

BELIEVE

I broke down and through all the crying and all the praying God said, "Son, I want you to start this ministry. I need you to do this. Will you trust Me?"

God gave me that Word. As I shared the story with the leaders in Raleigh, I explained my obedience to do what God told me to do even though I was scared and had many reservations was what ultimately led to my faith increasing. All of the success the ministry has had, all the lives that have been touched and all of the ways we have been able to make a difference, goes all the way back to my original act of obedience.

In the famous story of Peter walking on water, we often applaud the faith Peter had to get out of the boat. But what we miss is that his faith was a by-product of him being obedient to the Word of God.

Peter said, *"Lord if it's really You, bid me to come."*

Jesus gives him a Word and simply says, *"Come."*

Peter was the only one who responded in obedience to the Word, He got out of the boat, and started walking on water to Jesus. His faith was connected to his obedience.

Increasing Your Faith

When we feel like our faith is stagnant or we feel like we haven't heard God's voice in a while, we need to go back to the last thing He told us to do and ask ourselves, "Did we do it?" We not only have to hear the Word, but we have to heed it. We have to do what the Word tells us to do in order to increase our faith!

Many of us like to quote the passage from James 2, *"Faith without works is dead..."* but every time we see the word "works" or "deeds" we have to remember the literal translation from Greek to English is *"corresponding acts of obedience."* We're going to take another look at it with fresh eyes because what James is really saying is there is a connection between our faith and our corresponding acts of obedience. Let's read James 2:17-24:

> *"In the same way, faith by itself, if it is not accompanied by* [corresponding acts of obedience]*, is dead. But someone will say, "You have faith; I have deeds." Show me your faith without* [corresponding acts of obedience]*, and I will show you my faith by my* [corresponding acts of obedience]*. You believe that there is one God.*

BELIEVE

*Good! Even the demons believe that—and
shudder. You foolish person, do you want
evidence that faith without* [corresponding
acts of obedience] *is useless? Was not
our father Abraham considered righteous
for his* [corresponding acts of obedience]
*when he offered his son Isaac on the
altar? You see that his faith and his*
[corresponding acts of obedience] *were
working together, and his faith was made
complete by his* [corresponding acts of
obedience]. *And the scripture was fulfilled
that says, "Abraham believed God, and
it was credited to him as righteousness,"
and he was called God's friend. You see
that a person is considered righteous
by what they do* [corresponding acts of
obedience] *and not by faith alone."*

Now, back to the story I shared with the leaders in
Raleigh. They were struck by our willingness to give
everything up in order to obey God and plant the
church. They said, "Oh, you gave everything…"

82

Increasing Your Faith

I stopped them, "You have to know the beginning of the story. I grew up in the church and I came to the Lord at a young age but I did not really start living by faith until I was in graduate school. I remember the moment I was in King Chapel at Morehouse College. It was graduation day, and I was set to receive my Masters of Divinity Degree. After my master's degree, I was moving forward with the pursuit of my PhD.

I was pursuing the PhD, not because God told me to, but because I wanted job security. I was like, 'Listen Lord, I know you called me to ministry and all that but...I need a backup plan.'

My warped thinking was 'I don't want to be in a situation where I have to depend on the church financially'. My grandfather pastored two Baptist Churches as a career and as a result, growing up I saw all kinds of crazy things which made me very concerned about depending on church people for my livelihood.

BELIEVE

I said, 'Lord, I'll do the church 'thing' because I know that is what You want me to do, but I'm going to have some 'thing' else over here – the PhD program.' But on this particular day I was getting my Masters of Divinity and my family was in the stands and we were going to have a grand celebration after…but as I was sitting there waiting for my name to be called to walk the stage and get my degree – the conviction of the Lord hit my heart so strong.

The Lord said, 'When are you going to start trusting Me?'

I started crying and the people around me thought, 'Oh that's so sweet, tears of joy.'

Oh no, I was deeply convicted because here I was trying to teach the Bible but I was not heeding the Word. I was not trusting God. In that graduation ceremony, God was saying clearly, 'After all I've done for you, you still don't trust Me. When are you going to truly begin to live by faith and trust Me?'

Increasing Your Faith

I answered, crying, 'From this point on I will live by faith.' I got the degree and went to the celebration with my family.

A few weeks later, guess what, I was still doing the work to pursue the PhD, even though I told the Lord, I would trust Him. One day after my Greek class, my professor told me he wanted to recommend me for an opportunity that would send me Rome, Italy, with a delegation that would do some work at the Vatican.

He told me, 'This delegation is looking to identify two graduate students to go with them. They have already identified one graduate student and need an additional student; I think you would be great for it. I want to recommend you.'

I answered, 'Wow, okay." He interrupted, 'But here is the catch, you'll have to drop your PhD pursuits if you really want to go. You will be gone for a while and I don't believe you can do both things.'

BELIEVE

I thought, 'Hmmmm…' But remember I had promised God, 'Lord, I'm going to start living by faith. I'm going to start trusting You.' God provided the Word, so the necessary next step was the 'corresponding act of obedience.' I had to drop my PhD pursuits, in order to trust God, follow where He was leading and go to Italy!

Prior to this opportunity, I had never been out of the country before. My time in Italy was an incredible experience. While in Italy, I met an individual who was on the Board of The World Council of Churches.

She came to me and said, 'I'm really impressed by the work you've done here. The World Council of Churches is launching a new program in Germany, and I believe you would be great fit for the program. What if when you finish your time in Rome, you come to Germany?'

My initial thought was 'Germany? I don't know anyone in Germany! Why would I go to Germany?'

Once again, God reminded, 'But you said you were going to trust Me.'

So I went to Germany, and once again it was an incredible experience. When I came back to the U.S. I didn't know what to do next. I didn't have a job, I had dropped my PhD pursuits, so I began to pray, 'Lord, where do You want me to go?' I don't see an opportunity, I don't know where the next meal is coming from, I just don't know!'

A few weeks later, out of the blue, the phone rang, and it was a job offer. The offer was to move to South Florida to be the Executive Pastor of an incredible ministry.

Again I said to God, 'God, I don't know anyone in South Florida.'

God responded, 'You didn't know anyone in Italy, or Germany, either but in King Chapel you promised to trust Me.'

I moved to South Florida, and it was an incredible experience. It was there I met my wife and fell in love. In addition to being the Executive Pastor at a great ministry I also started a consulting business that was very successful.

BELIEVE

One day, I received a call from a Pastor in Birmingham, Alabama. He had heard about me and the work I did through my consulting business, and he invited me to come to Birmingham for some consulting work. What began as a consulting assignment in Birmingham led to me planting The Worship Center Christian Church.

That is how it began...but far more important than the places I had seen and the experiences I had, was me saying 'I'm going to trust You, God.'

Once I made that commitment God provided consistent opportunities for me to demonstrate my 'corresponding acts of obedience.' 'Will you drop the pursuit of the PhD?' (Corresponding act of obedience). 'Will you go to Rome?' (Corresponding act of obedience). 'Will you go to Germany?' (Corresponding act of obedience). 'Will you move to South Florida?' (Corresponding act of obedience).

Faith without 'corresponding acts of obedience' is dead! How do we increase our faith? First, hear the Word. Second, heed the Word. Third, the increase of faith is evident in how we pray.

The Increase of Faith Is Evident in How We Pray

As we hear and heed the Word, there will be evidence in how we pray of the faith increase in our hearts. Faith and prayer go together like a hand in a glove. It is impossible to teach the true essence of faith without understanding its connection to prayer.

In James 1:5-7, James tells us:

If any of you lacks wisdom, let him ask of God, who gives to all liberally and without reproach, and it will be given to him. But let him ask in faith, with no doubting, for he who doubts is like a wave of the sea driven and tossed by the wind. For let not that man suppose that he will receive anything from the Lord.

James is teaching us in these verses that all prayers are not answered. Only prayers prayed by faith are answered. Jesus has an interesting encounter in Matthew 17 that sheds more light on this truth. Jesus, Peter, James, and John are on the mountain of transfiguration.

BELIEVE

Jesus is transfigured. Peter, James, and John see Moses
and Elijah and come to understand Jesus as the
fulfillment of both the law and the prophets. Peter
thought it was all so amazing and wanted to build three
tabernacles and stay there.

Jesus told him, "No, we can't stay here, we need to
go back down the mountain." At the bottom of the
mountain was a problem. The problem was there was a
man whose son was demon-possessed and the disciples
were praying for this boy's healing but they were
ineffective. We pick up the story in Matthew 17:14-17:

> *At the foot of the mountain, a large crowd*
> *was waiting for them. A man came and*
> *knelt before Jesus and said, 'Lord, have*
> *mercy on my son. He has seizures and*
> *suffers terribly. He often falls into the fire*
> *or into the water. So I brought him to your*
> *disciples, but they couldn't heal him.'*
> *Jesus said, 'You faithless and corrupt*
> *people! How long must I be with you?*
> *How long must I put up with you? Bring*
> *the boy here to me.'*

Increasing Your Faith

It was a terrible rebuke to the disciples. What did the disciples do to deserve Jesus's response? It is difficult to understand until we dig into the etymology of the word "corrupt." It was a terrible rebuke to the disciples. What did the disciples do to deserve Jesus's response? It is difficult to understand until we dig into the etymology of the word "corrupt."

Jesus says, "you faithless and corrupt people." The word "corrupt" means "to cause someone to depart from correct behavior." When Jesus says "corrupt" He doesn't mean what we think of when we say "corrupt." He means corrupt in the sense that their (or our) faithlessness will cause believers to depart from correct behavior. When we are faithless we will do things we aren't supposed to do because we don't have faith. Without faith, we will act in ways we are not supposed to act.

Finishing the story, Matthew tells us in Matthew 17:19-21:

> *Afterward the disciples asked Jesus privately, 'Why couldn't we cast out that demon?'*

BELIEVE

'You don't have enough faith,' Jesus told them. 'I tell you the truth, if you had faith even as small as a mustard seed, you could say to this mountain, 'Move from here to there,' and it would move. Nothing would be impossible.'

After my consulting assignment was completed for the pastor in Birmingham, he asked me to remain over the weekend and speak at his church on Sunday. At the conclusion of service a man came up to me and said, "I perceive you to be a man of God." He continued, "My wife has had five miscarriages but I believe if you pray for her, God will touch her and she will become pregnant."

I prayed for her and she did become pregnant. In fact, they have had several children since then. Prior to this encounter, others had prayed for them, but they were unable to conceive.

This begs the question, "What made the difference?" The difference, I believe, was the faith in my heart. I knew the scriptures and I believed if God could do it for Sarah, Rebekah, and others, surely He could do it for this woman.

I didn't pray, "Well Lord if it is Your will," but "Lord, You laid it out in scripture…" so I prayed, "Lord, I know You are able, we want this womb be made whole." I prayed the way I prayed because faith was active in my heart.

In James 5:16, James tells us, *"The effective, <u>fervent</u> prayer of a righteous man avails much."* The truth of this verse is that an effective prayer is a fervent prayer and by correlation the opposite is true, a prayer that is not fervent is not effective. Fervent is not about how loud we get when we pray, or how active we act to exaggerate the power of God, it is not at all about any sort of church antics. Fervent is the passion in our hearts with which we pray because of how strongly we believe. Fervent is the faith in our hearts which says, "I'm not taking no for an answer because the Word of God says 'yes'." With that type of faith in our hearts, it results in passion (in fervor) in how we pray.

When active faith is in our hearts, it results in passion when we pray and creates a boldness found nowhere else. So, an effectual fervent prayer comes from a heart of faith!

BELIEVE

But if we are not hearing the Word of God on a consistent basis and we are not heeding the Word, then our faith will not increase and we will not be passionate when we pray. In other words, we will not pray an effectual fervent prayer.

When we aren't hearing the Word, heeding the Word, and increasing our faith, we will tolerate evil rather than hate evil. We will conform to the world instead of being transformed in our minds. We will end up going along with what everyone else is doing and saying instead of standing up for God and His Kingdom!

The book of Isaiah reveals one of the biggest issues God had with the nation of Israel, which led to them being sent into exile, was God's inability to find righteous people who would stand up and stand in the gap on behalf of the nation.

What He found instead were people going the wrong way, doing the wrong things, and saying the wrong things. They were His chosen people, they were supposed to be an example, but instead they were blending in and living like the other nations around them.

He looked for someone who would stand up for righteousness and holiness and purity, but he couldn't find anyone.

The same thing is happening today, and it has to change. One of the greatest tragedies today is the Church which should be "salt and light" is instead blending in and looking like everyone else. So many believers are going along with the culture around them, conforming to the world.

Hebrews 4:16 tells us to come boldly before the throne of grace but because faith is not increasing in our hearts, we don't go boldly before the throne of grace. It isn't a matter of praying, "Oh Lord, if it is Your will…" It is a matter of faith, believing what the Word of God says about purity, holiness, righteousness, and all His promises, and with that faith we can go boldly before God with our fervent prayers.

Think about it, we'll go crazy, shouting with passion galore at a college or NFL football game, rather than praying passionately to see God's kingdom happen on earth.

BELIEVE

While I enjoy football myself, the truth is, these coaches and teams are not going to clean up our communities, stop excessive killing in our neighborhoods, stop individuals from committing suicide, or fix a marriage or family. We need believers who can stand up and say, "I stand on the Word of God" so our fervent prayers can do all those things!

Look at the example James uses to describe effectual fervent prayer in James 5:16-18, *"The effective, fervent prayer of a righteous man avails much. Elijah was a man with a nature like ours, and he prayed earnestly that it would not rain; and it did not rain on the land for three years and six months. And he prayed again, and the heaven gave rain, and the earth produced its fruit."*

He is speaking of the events in 1 Kings 18, when God had shut up the heavens. In that passage when Elijah prayed for rain, he put his head between his knees, as God instructed. In this position, his heart was above his head.

Why? We often try to think our way into the things of God, but God wants us to have faith increasing in our hearts like Elijah.

Increasing Your Faith

Elijah wasn't thinking, logically reasoning, but rather, with his head out of the way, faith rose in his heart and he prayed, "Lord, You said it's going to rain and so I'm praying for rain, I'm here believing You." Even when his servant saw no sign of rain time after time, Elijah kept persistently praying.

If faith is increasing in our hearts, just because we don't see it right away, it doesn't mean God isn't going to do it. We have to keep praying fervently, with increasing faith as Jesus tells us in Luke 11:5-10:

> *Then Jesus said to them, 'Suppose you have a friend, and you go to him at midnight and say, 'Friend, lend me three loaves of bread; a friend of mine on a journey has come to me, and I have no food to offer him.' And suppose the one inside answers, 'Don't bother me. The door is already locked, and my children and I are in bed. I can't get up and give you anything.' ' I tell you, even though he will not get up and give you the bread because of friendship, yet because of your shameless audacity he will surely get up and give you as much as you need.*

BELIEVE

*So I say to you: Ask and it will be given to
you; seek and you will find; knock and the
door will be opened to you. For everyone
who asks receives; the one who seeks
finds; and to the one who knocks, the door
will be opened.*

In the Greek the verbs "ask, seek, and knock" are in
the tense that means to keep doing something, which
means not only asking, seeking, knocking a single time
– it means ask and keep asking, seek and keep seeking,
knock and keep knocking, and the doors will open to
you. It does not mean keep muttering empty phrases,
Jesus tells us this in Matthew 6:7, *"And when you pray,
do not heap up phrases (multiply words, repeating the
same ones over and over) as the Gentiles do, for they think
they will be heard for their much speaking."*

The point Jesus is making in Luke 11 is when faith is
in our hearts, we will have a passion and a boldness that
will not take "no" for an answer. What keeps us asking is
the passion in our hearts fueled by the increase of our
faith because we have heard the Word, we have heeded
the Word, and we believe what it says.

Increasing Your Faith

In Luke 18:1-8, Luke tells us:

*Then Jesus told his disciples a parable **to show them that they should always pray and not give up**. He said: 'In a certain town there was a judge who neither feared God nor cared what people thought. And there was a widow in that town who kept coming to him with the plea, 'Grant me justice against my adversary.'*

'For some time he refused. But finally he said to himself, 'Even though I don't fear God or care what people think, yet because this widow keeps bothering me, I will see that she gets justice, so that she won't eventually wear me out with her coming!'

And the Lord said, 'Listen to what the unjust judge says. And will not God bring about justice for his chosen ones, who cry out to him day and night? Will he keep putting them off? I tell you, he will see that they get justice, and quickly. However, when the Son of Man comes, will he find faith on the earth?'

Do we have increasing faith, the kind Jesus is looking for? The growing faith from hearing the Word, heeding the Word, and the increasing faith in our hearts which shows up in our bold, fervent prayers which avail much!

BELIEVE

Reflection

We can grow our faith, neglect our faith, or decrease our faith – which are you doing right now?

Why did Jesus warns His followers to be careful what they hear?

Why is it crucial to be in the Word daily?

What is the connection between faith and duty (obedience)?

What is the connection between faith and prayer?

Think of a time you went round and round with God - Write out a short synopsis of what God did to guide you onto the path He had for you and how your faith increased through it.

Chapter 4
Release Your Faith

" It is written: 'I believed; therefore I have spoken.' Since we have that same spirit of faith, we also believe and therefore speak."
~ 2 Corinthians 4:13

In the last chapter, we focused on increasing our faith, learning that what we hear affects what we believe and what we believe affects how we pray. Our faith is increased as we spend time hearing the Word of God and we believe.

In this chapter, we will learn that when our faith is increased, we then need to release it and in doing so we discover that what we believe affects what we speak. How do we do that?

We Release Our Faith as We Speak What We Believe

In 2 Corinthians 4:13, the Apostle Paul testifies that we release our faith when we speak our closely held beliefs, *"It is written: 'I believed; therefore I have spoken.' Since we have that same spirit of faith, we also believe and therefore speak."*

BELIEVE

It sounds simple, we speak what we believe. The same spirit of faith by which we live and walk is to be exercised when we speak what we believe. Jesus also taught this truth in Matthew 12:34, *"… For out of the abundance of the heart the mouth speaks."* What you believe is what comes out of your mouth. The problem which often arises in our consumption of 53 plus hours of screen "junk" each week is that unfortunately is what we so often speak. Why? It becomes the abundance of what is in our heart.

The same is true and very powerful when we are "consuming" the right things and in turn we grow in our faith. Faith becomes active and powerful when it is released. How is it released? It is released by the power of our words. Faith originates in our hearts as we read the word, study the word, and hear the word, and it is released by what we speak.

Romans 10:10 tells us, *"For with the heart one believes unto righteousness, and with the mouth confession is made unto salvation."*

Release Your Faith

It is the same principle. When we decided we wanted to accept Christ in our lives we believed – it was a heart decision. As a result of our belief, we confessed. The faith in our heart was evidenced by what we said – we confessed Jesus is Lord. The confession of faith brought salvation into our lives. We believed it and we spoke it. Our confession of Jesus released the faith to bring salvation into our hearts.

In Mark 11:22, Jesus is teaching about the connection between our faith and what we say when he explains, *"Jesus answered and said to them, 'Have faith in God.'"* *The literal translation from the Greek here is "have the faith of God."*

Jesus says, "Have faith in God (have the faith of God)." How does God operate? He speaks that which is not as though it already is. (See Genesis 1)

Continuing with Mark 11:22-23, *"So Jesus answered and said to them, 'Have faith in God. For assuredly, I say to you, whoever __says__ to this mountain, 'Be removed and be cast into the sea,' and does not doubt in his heart, but believes that those things he __says__ will be done, he will have whatever he __says__.'"*

BELIEVE

Do you see it? Jesus says, "Have faith in God," but then connects faith in God with what we say three times in this short passage.

He goes on in Mark 11:24, *"Therefore I say to you, whatever things you ask when you pray, believe that you receive them, and you will have them."* Jesus is doing two things. He is helping us understand that this notion of our faith being evidenced in what we say is undeniable. He goes on to say, "when you pray, then believe, and you will receive."

Faith is, "You believe, you pray, you speak, and then you will see!" The biblical way is "we believe because of what we have heard (His Word), we pray, we speak, and then we see.

Look back at the passage. Jesus doesn't say, "Ask the Father to move the mountain." He says, "You move the mountain by speaking to it!" Why does He say that? He tells us to speak to the mountain instead of telling us to pray, "Oh Father God, would you please move the mountain?" He tells us to speak to it to move it. Why?

Release Your Faith

Because God has given us the authority and we exercise that authority when we release our faith by what we speak!

Notice, when Jesus performed miracles, He didn't ask God to do it, He spoke to the issues Himself. In almost every miracle He performed, Jesus did not say, "Father would you please do it?" No, He spoke to the situation and it was done. Even when He gets to the grave of Lazarus, He says, "Dad, I thank You because You have already heard me," (John 11:41) but He doesn't pray, "Now Father would you raise Lazarus from the dead?" No, He goes to the grave of Lazarus and speaks to the situation, "Lazarus, come forth!" (John 11:43)

Some of you are thinking, "I need to check the record on this." I invite you to do so. Take a look at these examples and as you read each one notice the issue and how Jesus speaks to each one.

BELIEVE

- "When Jesus came down from the mountainside, large crowds followed him. A man with leprosy came and knelt before him and said, 'Lord, if you are willing, you can make me clean.' Jesus reached out his hand and touched the man. 'I am willing,' **he said**, 'Be clean!' Immediately he was cleansed of his leprosy" (Matthew 8:1-3).

- "When Jesus had entered Capernaum, a centurion came to him, asking for help. 'Lord,' he said, 'my servant lies at home paralyzed, suffering terribly.' Jesus said to him, 'Shall I come and heal him?' The centurion replied, 'Lord, I do not deserve to have you come under my roof. But just **say the word**, and my servant will be healed'... Then **Jesus said** to the centurion, 'Go! Let it be done just as you believed it would.' And his servant was healed at that moment" (Matthew 8:5-8, 13).

- "Then he got into the boat and his disciples followed him. Suddenly a furious storm came up on the lake, so that the waves swept over the boat. But Jesus was sleeping. The disciples went and woke him, saying, 'Lord, save us! We're going to drown!' He replied, 'You of little faith, why are you so afraid?' Then he got up and **rebuked the winds** and the waves, and it was completely calm" (Matthew 8:23-26).

- *"Jesus stepped into a boat, crossed over and came to his own town. Some men brought to him a paralyzed man, lying on a mat. When Jesus saw their faith, **he said** to the man, 'Take heart, son; your sins are forgiven.' At this, some of the teachers of the law said to themselves, 'This fellow is blaspheming!' Knowing their thoughts, Jesus said, 'Why do you entertain evil thoughts in your hearts? Which is easier to say, 'Your sins are forgiven,' or to say, 'Get up and walk'? But I want you to know that the Son of Man has authority on earth to forgive sins.' So **he said** to the paralyzed man, 'Get up, take your mat and go home.'" (Matthew 9:1-6).*

- *"When they came to the crowd, a man approached Jesus and knelt before him. 'Lord, have mercy on my son,' he said. 'He has seizures and is suffering greatly. He often falls into the fire or into the water. I brought him to your disciples, but they could not heal him.' 'You unbelieving and perverse generation,' Jesus replied, 'how long shall I stay with you? How long shall I put up with you? Bring the boy here to me.' **Jesus rebuked the demon**, and it came out of the boy, and he was healed at that moment"* (Matthew 17:14-18).

BELIEVE

- "They went to Capernaum, and when the Sabbath came, Jesus went into the synagogue and began to teach. The people were amazed at his teaching because he taught them as one who had authority, not as the teachers of the law. Just then a man in their synagogue who was possessed by an impure spirit cried out, 'What do you want with us, Jesus of Nazareth? Have you come to destroy us? I know who you are—the Holy One of God!' '<u>Be quiet!</u>' **said Jesus sternly.** "<u>Come out of him</u>!' The impure spirit shook the man violently and came out of him with a shriek" (Mark 1:21-26).

- "Jesus left the synagogue and went to the home of Simon. Now Simon's mother-in-law was suffering from a high fever, and they asked Jesus to help her. So he bent over her and **<u>rebuked the fever</u>**, and it left her. She got up at once and began to wait on them" (Luke 4:38-39).

- *"Soon afterward, Jesus went to a town called Nain, and his disciples and a large crowd went along with him. As he approached the town gate, a dead person was being carried out—the only son of his mother, and she was a widow. And a large crowd from the town was with her. When the Lord saw her, his heart went out to her and he said, 'Don't cry.' Then he went up and touched the coffin they were carrying him on, and the bearers stood still. **He said**, 'Young man, I say to you, get up!' (Luke 7:11-14).*

- *"As Jesus approached Jericho, a blind man was sitting by the roadside begging. When he heard the crowd going by, he asked what was happening. They told him, 'Jesus of Nazareth is passing by.' He called out, 'Jesus, Son of David, have mercy on me!' Those who led the way rebuked him and told him to be quiet, but he shouted all the more, 'Son of David, have mercy on me!' Jesus stopped and ordered the man to be brought to him. When he came near, Jesus asked him, 'What do you want me to do for you?' 'Lord, I want to see,' he replied. **Jesus said to him**, 'Receive your sight; your faith has healed you.' Immediately he received his sight and followed Jesus, praising God. When all the people saw it, they also praised God" (Luke 18:35-43).*

BELIEVE

Jesus said, He spoke, He rebuked – He exercised authority and spoke to each situation and it was.

There was a couple in Hawaii who were pastors. Their son had a rare degenerative eye disease. It is so rare that very few people get but it leads to blindness in a short period of time.

The asked their church to pray with them as they fasted and prayed. They called friends and family members around the world who were believers and invited them to fast and pray as well.

One morning, the husband was in his prayer/ devotional time reading the Word when he received a similar revelation about Jesus. He came out and told his wife, "Honey I think we are doing this all wrong."

She asked, "What do you mean?" He answered, "I know prayer is powerful and it changes things, but I'm recognizing that we have to release our faith and speak to the situation. We've been praying for God to heal but the Word of God says, "…by His stripes we are healed." (Isaiah 53:5) God has already provided for the healing of our son but we now have to start speaking it."

Release Your Faith

It is what they began to do. Literally, they started speaking God's healing over their son. Every day they would speak God's Word over their son, "He's healed, he's healed, he's healed."

Then it came time to return to the doctor. The first stop during the appointment was radiology, followed by a visit with the doctor who had the results. The doctor, looking at the scan, began by apologizing, "I'm sorry, I believe radiology made a mistake when they did the scan. I'm going to have to send you back to repeat the scan."

They returned and the scan was repeated. The doctor got the scan and once again they met with him. He said, "Oh my goodness, I just don't understand. I don't know what is going on today. This has never happened before, I'm so sorry. I'm going to have to send you back again because there is something wrong with the scan."

They repeated the scan a third time. The family returned and the doctor, scan in hand, started, "I'm so sorry, I'm embarrassed, we've never had this problem. I'm going to escort you all back to radiology and do the scan myself."

BELIEVE

He took them back and did the scan himself. Looking at the fourth scan, he said, "I don't understand because the disease is no longer there. The scan is not picking it up."

The father said, "I understand. We started speaking the Word of God, declaring our faith, and releasing it over our son and 'by His stripes he is healed!'"

Prayer is extremely powerful but we release our faith when we begin to speak the Word of God over our situation.

Some of you may be asking, "How is that possible?" How?

Spiritual laws supersede natural laws.

Spiritual Laws Supersede Natural Laws

As we dive into this truth, let's answer the question, "What is a law?"

Release Your Faith

Webster's defines law as "that which is laid, set or fixed, or "a principle based on predictable consequences of an act." For example, the Law of Gravity, a natural law discovered by Sir Isaac Newton, basically says "what goes up must come down." He also discovered the weight of an object determines how quickly gravity will pull it down. So, if you are at the top of a building you can determine how quickly the object you are about to drop will take to reach the ground. Why? The Law of Gravity is a principle based on the predictable consequences of an act.

Nevertheless, the Law of Gravity can be superseded by the Law of Lift, the Law of Thrust, the Law of Drag, and other natural laws. When pilots are learning to fly, they understand that while gravity is real, there are others laws higher than gravity, laws which supersede it. The Law of Lift, the Law of Thrust, and the Law of Drag states than when an airplane, no matter its size, reaches a certain speed (Thrust) and the pilot pulls back tilting the nose up (Lift), the plane will take off and stay in the air to get the plane where it needs to go. It is how airplanes fly, thus superseding the law of gravity.

BELIEVE

Just as there are natural laws which supersede other natural laws, there are spiritual laws which supersede natural laws.

A great spiritual law which supersedes natural law is Proverbs 18:21 which warns, *"The tongue has the power of life and death, and those who love it will eat its fruit."* Literally it means our words determine our life, our fate. Our fate is not determined by the enemy, society, or our circumstances, it is determined by our words. When we believe the Word of God and speak the Word of God, we release a force to which everything else in the universe **must adjust**!

How is this even possible? It is possible because everything in the natural world came from the spiritual world.

Jesus explains in John 4:24, "God is spirit, and his worshipers must worship in the Spirit and in truth." God is spirit, and yet He created the entire physical universe. Everything we encounter in this physical, natural world came from the spiritual world of God. Everything we connect with through our physical senses – sight, hearing, taste, touch, smell – came from God.

The writer of Hebrews in Hebrews 11:3 writes, *"By faith, we see the world called into existence by God's word, what we see created by what we don't see."* Everything in the physical, natural world was created by the spiritual world, by the Word of God! It is worth repeating, everything in the natural world was created by God and His Word. Spiritual laws supersede natural laws!

It is the reason Jesus says in Mark 11, *"Have faith in God."* It literally means, "Have the faith of God." He is saying have the faith of God – God stepped into nothing and started speaking, "Let there be light." (Genesis 1:3) Light did not exist before this, but light had to come into existence because he spoke it. Take some time to read through Genesis 1. Everything is the Word. "And God said…and it was…" over and over again. It is the whole creation account. It is the Word that does the work. Everything we come into contact with came into existence because the Word of God created it. Spiritual laws supersedes natural laws.

BELIEVE

John explains in John 1:1-3, *"In the beginning was the Word, and the Word was with God, and the Word was God. He was with God in the beginning. Through him all things were made; without him nothing was made that has been made."* Everything was made through the Word.

John is gently reminding us that in Genesis 1:1, the Word did all the work! God gave Adam and Eve and all humanity the same ability and authority through the power of His Word! We are created in the image and likeness of God. The image and likeness is not about appearance, but about function, the ability God gave us. Just as He created with His Word, He has given us that same ability to create through His Word.

Satan, the enemy, knows the power of God's Word and that is why he slithers into the Garden of Eden and sin enters the world. How? His goal was to get them to doubt the Word of God. Remember what he asked them, "Did God really say…"

Release Your Faith

We are created in the image and likeness of God too, and we have the same ability and authority over evil though the power of His Word. He wanted them to doubt God's Word because he knows God's power. It is the same strategy Satan uses on us today. He tries to get us to doubt the Word of God. Why? If we doubt the Word of God, we won't really believe God's Word. If we don't believe God's Word, we won't pray His Word. If we won't pray the Word of God, then we won't speak His Word.

The enemy knows if we start believing the Word of God, praying the Word of God, and speaking the Word of God, then everything in our lives will begin shifting and changing according to the Word of God. Everything about the way the world is set up and operating today is designed to get us to doubt the Word of God. Think about all the questions the world is posing to us. "Did God really say that about marriage? Did God really say that about parenting? Did God really say that about money?" The enemy knows just how powerful the Word of God is! The moment we start releasing our faith – believing His Word, praying His Word, and speaking His Word – the enemy knows there is nothing He can do to stop God's power.

BELIEVE

When we begin to look at something and we are not moved by how it looks but we declare the Word of God unto that situation – the enemy knows things are going to start changing and coming together!

Adam and Eve gave up the authority God had given them, but Jesus, the second Adam, came and restored to us the authority Adam and Eve lost. Jesus tells us in Matthew 12:36-37, *"But I tell you that everyone will have to give account on the day of judgment for every empty word they have spoken. For by your words, you will be acquitted, and by your words you will be condemned."*

Read it again from The Message, *"Let me tell you something: Every one of these careless words is going to come back to haunt you. There will be a time of Reckoning. Words are powerful; take them seriously. Words can be your salvation. Words can also be your damnation."*

We will have to give account for every careless word we speak because words are powerful. In John 6:63, Jesus says, *"My words are spirit and they are life."*

Every time we speak words which are not in line with the Word of God, the enemy wins! Every time we speak the Word of God in our situation, things change for the better! There is nothing in the universe so big and powerful that it cannot be changed when we speak the Word of God!

The psalmist warns us in Psalm 141:3, "Set a guard over my mouth, Lord; keep watch over the door of my lips." He is asking God to help him not to mess up with his mouth. He is asking God to make sure his mouth is in line with God's Truth. Isn't it interesting how we can pray for a breakthrough and then talk ourselves right out of it?

The psalmist also testifies in Psalm 39:1, *"I said, "I will watch my ways and keep my tongue from sin; I will put a muzzle on my mouth while in the presence of the wicked."* We have to watch our associations because they will try to make us feel comfortable about saying things that are not only wrong but flat out against the Word of God.

BELIEVE

In Ephesians 1:3, Paul writes, *"Praise be to the God and Father of our Lord Jesus Christ, who has blessed us in the heavenly realms with every spiritual blessing in Christ."* The Word does not tell us God is going to do it but rather that God has already blessed us. God is the Alpha and Omega, the first and the last, the beginning and the end. He has already worked it all out. He has already gone ahead of us. We are never in a situation which surprises God. Nothing ever dawns on God. Wherever we find ourselves, it is not a surprise to God. He has already worked out whatever we need for where we are and where we are going! God has already blessed in the heavenly realms with every spiritual blessing in Christ.

So how do we tap into what God has already done, these blessings already done in the heavenly realms? We do so by releasing our faith and by speaking what God says in His Word about your situation!

For example, if we say, "I don't have any peace!" then we have just disagreed with the Word in Ephesians 1:3.

Instead of saying, "I don't have any peace," we should have declared Romans 5:1, *"Therefore, since we have been justified through faith, we have peace with God through our Lord Jesus Christ,"* and tapped directly into what God has already done in heaven and so manifest it on the earth! We should change our declaration and thank God for the peace we already have and then decree that peace in the situation. Making that declaration taps into what God has already done in the heavenlies and manifest it on the earth.

Everything we will ever need in our life God has already done in heaven, but what brings it from heaven to earth are the words we speak! It is a big challenge for many of us because the world has programmed us to speak based on what we see. But we are created by God to speak His Word until His Word becomes what we see. We are to speak what we believe until we see what we believe. God's Word says if we decree it, it shall be established. (Job 22:28)

BELIEVE

We don't say what we see (as the world does), we say what we believe (as the Word does) until what we believe is what we see. God has so much He has already ordained for us, but the only person who can stop us from attaining it is ourselves.

No man, no principality or power, no government, no class or system, nothing and no one can stop us from tapping into what God has for us except us! The only person who can get in the way of what God has for us is us. It is not about anyone else, but all about what we believe and what we speak!

Remember in Ezekiel 37, when God placed Ezekiel in the Valley of Dry Bones and asked, "Ezekiel, can these bones live?" That was the test!

Ezekiel answered, "Lord, only you know."

We are so quick to put our mouth on a situation to say it is dead, so messed up no one can do anything when what we should be saying is, "Lord, only you know."

We need to get our copy of the Word and get our verse and start speaking that Word into the "dry, dead" situation.

God told Ezekiel to prophesy to the bones. Prophesy means to "speak that which is not as though it were." When Ezekiel began to prophesy to the bones, the bones began coming together, things started changing. We need to do the same, prophesy to our situation, to our marriage, to our children, to our communities…"thus says the Word of the Lord."

Recently, God has convicted me on this, telling me I need to declare what I am praying. For example, I pray for my marriage and my children daily, but I don't always "prophesy" declaring God's promises over them. God led me to Psalm 112:1-2, which reads, "*Praise the Lord. Blessed are those who fear the Lord, who find great delight in his commands. Their children will be mighty in the land; the generation of the upright will be blessed.*"

BELIEVE

As I read the Word, I knew I believed, I knew I feared the Lord, I knew I found delight in Him, so after my prayer was finished, I began walking through the house, declaring "my children will be mighty in this land" and then I said, "I thank You that Your hand is on my children and that You are going to do something mighty through them."

As I continued declaring, the Holy Spirit spoke once more and Holy Spirit directed me to Deuteronomy 28:1-13 in regard to what I have been praying for our church. I read:

> *If you fully obey the Lord your God and*
> *carefully follow all his commands I give*
> *you today, the Lord your God will set*
> *you high above all the nations on earth.*
> *All these blessings will come on you and*
> *accompany you if you obey the Lord your*
> *God: You will be blessed in the city and*
> *blessed in the country...Your basket and*
> *your kneading trough will be blessed...*
> *You will be blessed when you come in*
> *and blessed when you go out...The LORD*
> *will send a blessing on your barns and on*
> *everything you put your hand to.*

Release Your Faith

I knew God was prompting me to declare His Word and I did, "I will be blessed in the city and in the country…I will be blessed when I come in and when I go out…everything I put my hands to will be blessed."

We have to pray – prayer is powerful. But the time comes when we have to declare…to speak God's Word into our lives, our situations – "thus says the Lord." We have to declare God's Word over our family, our children, our finances, our everything to tap into its power.

If we don't believe it, we can't pray it. If we can't pray it, we can't declare it. We have to release our faith to say what we believe until we see it! We have to declare His favor, His blessing. We have to release words which are in line with scripture. There is power in His Word. His Word, if we believe it and we release it – just like the Word brought the world into existence – the Word will begin to change our situation.

BELIEVE

In Acts 3 Peter and John had gone to the temple to pray, and a man at the gate asked them for money. In verses 4-8, we read how they responded:

> *Peter looked straight at him, as did John. Then Peter said, 'Silver or gold I do not have, but what I have I give you. In the name of Jesus Christ of Nazareth, walk'. Taking him by the right hand, he helped him up, and instantly the man's feet and ankles became strong. He jumped to his feet and began to walk. Then he went with them into the temple courts, walking and jumping and praising God.*

This passage reminds us that we have to stop seeing what we don't have and instead start declaring what we do have in Him. We have to release our faith and declare the Word of God over our situation, knowing God has already provided for us.

Reflection

Jesus taught this truth in Matthew 12:34, *"... For out of the abundance of the heart the mouth speaks."* Think about the words you speak. Does this verse make you say "ouch" because what you have been speaking obviously isn't from God?

Read Genesis 1 and note every time God said and it was.

Read in Genesis 3 how Satan got Adam and Eve to doubt God's Word – what similar tactic has he used on you to get you to doubt God's Word?

"Words can be your salvation. Words can also be your damnation" (Matthew 12:36-37 (MSG)). Are you using your words for your salvation or your damnation?

What have you been praying that you need to believe for, declare, and speak?

Chapter 5
The Confession That Brings Victory

"The Spirit gives life; the flesh counts for nothing. The words I have spoken to you are spirit and they are life"
~ John 6:63

We know the Bible says, "Faith comes by hearing and hearing by the Word of God" so we hear with our minds but the more we hear the Word of God the more it takes root in our hearts and impacts what we believe. We know what we believe effects how we pray and in turn, what we believe effects what we speak. All of this increases our faith.

In the last chapter we learned that once our faith is increased we release our faith by speaking what we believe. We also came to understand God has already provided for us, we just need to pray and declare His Word over our situation or circumstance. We also discovered everything in the physical world in which we interact was spoken into being by the Word which means spiritual laws always supersede natural laws.

BELIEVE

In this chapter, we will continue to learn to release our faith as we explore the confession which brings victory.

The Confession That Brings Victory

What we hear affects what we believe. What we believe affects how we pray and what we speak. We release our faith when we speak what we believe.

Words have spiritual power. They are not to be taken lightly. Jesus testified to this truth in John 6:63 when He said, *"The Spirit gives life; the flesh counts for nothing. The words I have spoken to you—they are full of the Spirit and life."*

He says, *"the flesh counts for nothing…but my words are full of Spirit and life."* It is a profound truth with which we need to wrestle and grasp because most of us live our life by virtue of the flesh, the way the world has led us to live life. Jesus is telling us when it comes to the kingdom of God, His truths, and His promises, our flesh has little or nothing to do with it.

The Confession That Brings Victory

He tells us His Words are Spirit and life, yet most of us have not made the connection between what we say and what we have in life. Many still have no idea the two are closely connected.

As believers, many of us don't understand that our words are spiritual and powerful especially when we are speaking the Word of God. Why? There are a lot of faulty beliefs in the world and in the body of Christ around the area of declaration and confession.

The faulty beliefs come from two pervasive ideas we are bombarded with in the world. For example, a lot of people think confession is limited to crime, that is, when someone commits a crime and then ultimately they confess. We see it in a lot of the entertainment we watch and books we read in which the plot narrative is built around a crime having been committed and the police trying to get a confession.

Another common understanding of the word confession is rooted in Catholicism – when a person commits a wrongdoing, he or she must go to a priest to confess.

BELIEVE

Part of the inability for us to fully grasp and apply what Jesus says in John 6:63 are these two pervasive ideas regarding confession in our culture. The problem with both of these is they are negative and it has led to our tendency to think about confession in a very negative way. In many ways we have been programmed to think confession is all about crime and sin and that in general, confession is a bad thing, but it is not true. In order to help us discern the truth we need to know and understand the four types of Biblical Confession.

The 4 Types of Biblical Confessions

The Confession of Sin

We read about the confession of sin in Mark 1:4-5, when Mark writes, *"And so John the Baptist appeared in the wilderness, preaching a baptism of repentance for the forgiveness of sins. The whole Judean countryside and all the people of Jerusalem went out to him. Confessing their sins, they were baptized by him in the Jordan River."* This is the confession people made when they came to John the Baptist to be baptized by him.

The Confession That Brings Victory

John was the precursor to Jesus on purpose. The first thing that must happen is a confession of sin. If we don't confess that we are inadequate, that we are sinners, then we can never get to the point in which we recognize we need a savior. The confession of sin is an acknowledgement that we are sinners, and we need a savior. We cannot save ourselves.

The Confession of the Lordship of Jesus Christ (The Confession for Salvation)

The confession of the Lordship of Jesus Christ is described in Romans 10:9-10, *"If you declare with your mouth, 'Jesus is Lord,' and believe in your heart that God raised him from the dead, you will be saved. For it is with your heart that you believe and are justified, and it is with your mouth that you profess your faith and are saved."* This is the confession of a sinner acknowledging Jesus as Lord. It is also acknowledging that we want Him in our lives and we want to submit to Him and to His Lordship (He is Lord of all). It is accepting that He needs to reign in our lives and lead. It is not about us leading our own lives. This is the confession that is the pre-requisite for salvation. If there is no confession, there is no salvation.

BELIEVE

When we confess Jesus Christ as Lord, we become new individuals as explained in 2 Corinthians 5:17, *"Therefore, if anyone is in Christ, the new creation has come: The old has gone, the new is here!"* With this confession, all sins are forgiven (past, present, and future) and the Holy Spirit takes up residence in us as we become a member of the family of believers. **This is the most important confession any of us will make in our lifetime. It changes our eternal destiny and the very essence of who we are.**

The Confession of Restoring Fellowship

John describes the confession of restoring fellowship in 1 John 1:9, *"If we confess our sins, he is faithful and just and will forgive us our sins and purify us from all unrighteousness."* This confession is made by us as believers when we find ourselves out of fellowship with God because we have disobeyed the Word of God or the Holy Spirit, or because of sinful decisions or actions. It is the confession we are to make when we sin and "transgress." The etymology the word "transgressions" means "to miss the mark." Transgression comes when we sin and get outside of the plans God has mapped out for our lives and our future. When we transgress beyond God's plan for our lives, we miss the mark.

The Confession That Brings Victory

The truth is we all miss the mark sometimes. It doesn't matter how anointed we are, how gifted we are, or how degreed or accomplished we are. We all miss the mark. When we confess those times whether we are clearly aware of them or have completely overlooked them, we are telling God we don't want anything to hinder our relationship (fellowship) with Him.

The good news is as children of God, forgiveness and cleansing are always available to us. When we confess our sins, God not only immediately forgives us, but He also immediately forgets our sins. How can we be sure? He promises to do so in Psalm 103:12, *"as far as the east is from the west, so far has he removed our transgressions from us."*

God doesn't pull skeletons out of our closet nor does He pull out a list and start calling the roll of our sins.

No, His Word promises our transgressions are removed from us, as far as the east is from the west. He reminds us of His promise again and again like the pledge in Jeremiah 31:34b, *"For I will forgive their wickedness and will remember their sins no more."*

BELIEVE

The Confession That Brings Victory

As believers, many of us know nothing about this confession. In fact, this is the confession the enemy doesn't want us to know about because it is a powerful confession. This confession is about speaking the Word of God in faith. It is not about speaking pop psychology, pop culture, or social media fads. It is all about releasing our faith and speaking the Word of God. Paul describes it in Romans 10:10, *"For with the heart one believes unto righteousness, and with the mouth <u>confession</u> is made unto salvation."*

In this verse, the Greek word translated as "confession" is *homologeo*. It is a compound word: homo means "same" and *logeo* means "word," thus *homologeo* means "to say the same word, or the same thing as another, to agree with."

For us, as believers, this "confession" or *homologeo* means to say the same word or the same thing God says, to agree with God, to say what He says in His Word. We should be agreeing with God and saying what He has already said in His Word. That is *homologeo*.

The Confession That Brings Victory

It is exactly why Paul tells us in Ephesians 4: 29-31, *"Do not let any unwholesome talk come out of your mouths, but only what is helpful for building others up according to their needs, that it may benefit those who listen. And do not grieve the Holy Spirit of God, with whom you were sealed for the day of redemption. Get rid of all bitterness, rage and anger, brawling and <u>slander</u>, along with every form of malice."*

Paul says we shouldn't let anything come out of our mouths except that which is useful for building others up and we should not grieve the Holy Spirit. When we let words come out of our mouths which are not *homologeo* (agreeing with God and saying what He has already said in His Word), the Holy Spirit is grieved.

We are not to tear people down with our words but build them up. Slander means to make a false and damaging statement about someone, even ourselves. Yes, we sometimes slander even ourselves when we fail to agree with what the Word of God says about us, His children.

BELIEVE

Every time we do, the Holy Spirit is grieved. It makes
no difference what the circumstance or situation might
look like in the natural realm, we have to look past it
and say what God says! What God says should always be
our confession!

Why Should This Be Our Confession?

**God has never said anything that didn't come to
pass.** The benefit of saying what God says can be found
in Numbers 23:19, where Moses explains, *"God is not
man, one given to lies, and not a son of man changing his
mind. Does he speak and not do what he says? Does he
promise and not come through?"* Moses's questions are
rhetorical. He knows this is not the God we serve. God
is not like your family members, your friends, your co-
workers.

God does NOT lie. He does what He says He is going
to do and His promises always come through! Paul
testifies to it in 1 Thessalonians 5:24, *"The One who
called you is completely dependable. If he said it, he'll do
it!"*

The Confession That Brings Victory

This is the reason we need to speak what we believe and say what He said, because if He said it, He will do it!

God has already laid out the path for you. God confirms this truth in Isaiah 46:10, *"I make known the end from the beginning, from ancient times, what is still to come. I say, 'My purpose will stand, and I will do all that I please."* As humans, we work from the beginning to the end. God doesn't work like that. God works from the end. He has already gone ahead of us, working everything out. Wherever we are – our struggles, our problems, our unknown – is not a surprise to God. He has already seen it and He has already gone up ahead of us and made provision for the challenge that may be a surprise to you but not to Him. Another reason for us to say what He says when we get into issues.

God has told us from the beginning what will be, He has never stopped letting us know what is going to happen, He will do exactly what He originally set out to do.

We don't have to fear He will abandon us. We don't have to worry because He has promised to be with us for the long haul. God has already seen our future and in the end, we win!

BELIEVE

He has already set the path before us and we need to follow that path. We don't have to look for new paths to follow. We travel the path successfully with our words. We have to take accountability for what we speak and hold others accountable as well. How do we miss this? We don't realize where our words go.

Where Our Words Go

Our words go somewhere. When we speak God's Word, things are set into motion that we can't see with our natural eyes but they are real and they are powerful. In Hebrews 3:1, we read, *"Therefore, holy brethren, partakers of the heavenly calling, consider the Apostle and High Priest of our <u>confession</u>, Christ Jesus."*

The book of Hebrews, remember, is a commentary, a bridge, between the Old Covenant and the New Covenant.

The writer of Hebrews is addressing New Covenant believers (us) and he wants us to understand the meaning of the Old Covenant and to comprehend the reality of the New Covenant and what we now have through Jesus Christ.

The Confession That Brings Victory

Now, let's break this verse down. "Holy brothers" is us, believers, followers of Christ, and our "heavenly calling" is to establish God's will on earth as it is in heaven. If you are asking, "How do we do that?" You are not alone, even though you probably already know the answer.

In our sphere of influence, whoever we are and whatever we do, our kingdom calling is to establish the will of God on earth as it is in heaven. It is what we are called to do as a church. We establish God's will on earth by doing what God called us to do for His glory.

He is our "High Priest," to whom we "confess." In the Old Testament, the people would bring all their offerings to the High Priest and confess their sins.

The High Priest, on the Day of Atonement, would take all their offerings, their requests, and their confessions and go into the Holy of Holies (where the presence of God was). He wore the Ephod and Breastpiece, which had the twelve stones representing the twelve tribes of Israel and went before God on behalf of the people. It was the Old Testament way.

BELIEVE

For us, New Covenant believers, when we speak words, our words don't fall to the ground, but our words go directly to Jesus in heaven. The Bible says He is our ultimate High Priest who lives to make intercession for us (Hebrews 7:25). He is at the right hand of God the Father Almighty and when we speak our words, our words go to Him. He then, takes our words to the Father. It is why when we pray, we deliver our prayers in the name of Jesus. Why? Because our prayers go directly to Him!

The problem is our words are not the only words Jesus hears in heaven. In Revelation 12:9-11, John tells us:

The great dragon was hurled down—that ancient serpent called the devil, or Satan, who leads the whole world astray. He was hurled to the earth, and his angels with him. Then I heard a loud voice in heaven say: "Now have come the salvation and the power and the kingdom of our God, and the authority of his Messiah. For the accuser of our brothers and sisters, who accuses them before our God day and night, has been hurled down. They triumphed over him by the blood of the Lamb and by the word of their testimony...

The Confession That Brings Victory

Right now, in heaven, Satan is making accusations to God about us day and night. We know it is true because it is exactly what happened to Job. (See Job 1:6) Just like then, right now there is a trial going on in heaven before God as Satan makes accusations about us.

At the same time Jesus hears us when we make our confession of faith. The Bible says we overcome Satan by the blood of the Lamb and the word of our testimony which means our confession of the Word of God by faith. (Revelation 12:11)

John, in 1 John 2:1, also tells us, *"My little children, these things I write to you, so that you may not sin. And if anyone sins, we have an Advocate with the Father, Jesus Christ the righteous."* Jesus is our advocate. The word means "attorney." Jesus is our "defense attorney."

Allow me to paint a picture of what is happening in heaven right now. The devil is making his case against us day and night. He makes his case, "They are no good, God. They are not worthy to be your children. They are wretched. They are guilty, God. They haven't done what you told them to do. They are guilty."

BELIEVE

As the prosecution rests, God, the Judge, turns to Jesus, our Advocate, and says, "I would like to hear from the defense now." We have an advocate, a defense attorney, who is better than Johnnie Cochran, Willie Gary, F. Lee Bailey, and Robert Shapiro!

Jesus responds, "I call my blood to the stand to testify." The blood of Jesus takes the stand and testifies that we are forgiven, cleansed, made righteous, and innocent because His blood paid the price for our sins.

But the Judge is not yet satisfied. The testimony of the blood alone does not settle it. Why? Revelation 12:11 explains, Jesus has the witness of His blood, but he needs another witness – the word of our testimony!

Our life is on trial and many of us are losing the case because our words do not testify for us! Many of us are taking the stand and instead of testifying in a way that will help our defense, our words align with the prosecution. We speak negatively, "it's never going to happen, I'm no good, I can't accomplish it."

The enemy says, "See God I told You."

Our Advocate asks, "What in the world is going on?"

The Confession That Brings Victory

We should be saying, "We can do all things through Christ who gives me strength. We are the lender and not the borrower. We are blessed and highly favored. We are the head and not the tail. We are blessed going out and coming in."

We should be testifying to His Word, His promises. Why? The Word tells us in Matthew 12:37, *"For by your words you will be acquitted, and by your words you will be condemned."*

Acquitted means "not guilty." Condemned means put in bondage and imprisoned. The blood has already testified on our behalf but the final witness is our word of confession. We have to say what the Word says! "Let the weak say I am strong. Let the poor say I am rich" (Joel 3:10). We need to say what the Word says! "We are blessed, we are heirs, we can do all things. There is no good thing He will withhold if we walk uprightly" (Philippians 4:13, Psalm 84:11).

Many of us need to fix "our mouths!" Many of us are in bondage, in prison, and condemned. Why?

BELIEVE

It is what happens to us when our words don't testify for us and say the same thing God says about us. It's interesting that we spend so much time talking about the blood, yet we only have it half right, we also need to make sure that the "word of our testimony" helps us instead of hinders us. We have to say the same thing that the Word of God says.

Reflection

If you have made the following confessions which lead to victory, tell someone close to you about the experience.

The Confession of Sin

The Confession of Salvation (Lordship of Jesus Christ)

The Confession of Restoring Fellowship

The Confession that Brings Victory

Where do your words go?

What are your words testifying about you?

Chapter 6
The Testing of Faith

"My brethren, count it all joy when you fall into various trials, knowing that <u>the testing of your faith</u> produces patience. But let patience have its perfect work, that you may be perfect and complete, lacking nothing."
~ James 1:2-4

We have covered a great deal in our reading and study so far. In this chapter, we will delve into how to face the testing of our faith.

In 2014, General Motors (GM) had to recall more than 39 million vehicles because the cars, trucks, and sport utility vehicles in question had not been thoroughly tested. The result - a number of deaths were linked to faulty ignition switches – and GM had to pay hefty fines to the families of those who lost their lives as a result. The judge in the case ordered them to pay millions to families who lost loved ones. In addition, the company sustained serious damage to their credibility as a brand as people around the world who once trusted GM lost faith in the once-reputable car company.

BELIEVE

The tragic loss of life could have been avoided, the millions paid in damages could have been avoided, and the hit to their brand could have been avoided had GM simply put their vehicles through the proper testing process. This true story proves how vitally important a good testing process is.

It's not only true for car manufacturers but also for each of us. God is completely committed to our faith being real. It makes sense because we know "without faith it is impossible to please God." We know, as believers, "the just shall live by faith."

God is so intentional and so committed to our faith being genuine, not counterfeit, that He will not release us into our next step of purpose, our next step of opportunity, and our next step of destiny until He knows we are ready. How does He know? He determines our readiness by testing our faith. Why? **A faith that has not been tested is not real faith at all!**

Mike Tyson, former world heavyweight champion, famously said, "Everyone has a plan until they get punched in the mouth!" While it is true for boxing, there are some nuggets there which relate to us as we study faith.

The Testing of Faith

Many of us say we have faith, until our faith is tested ("get punched in the mouth"). In fact, it is the main reason James wrote his epistle (letter) to the Jewish Christians.

Each of the New Testament letters have their own unique theme, purpose, and audience. Paul wrote Romans to prepare the Church and the believers in Rome for his first visit. He wrote what we know as 1st Corinthians to the Church at Corinth to help them address and correct issues they were experiencing. Paul penned Galatians to a group of churches warning them against growing legalism and false teachings in their midst.

Likewise, James writes this epistle to a group of believers who were having problems in their personal lives and in their church fellowship. They were experiencing multiple and difficult tests of their faith and the tests were the source of their problems.

The more information James received about their problems helped him recognize the foundation, the root cause of their problems was spiritual immaturity. They were simply not "growing up" spiritually.

BELIEVE

It is the reason the book we now know as James is primarily focused on spiritual maturity. James opens his letter (James 1:2-4) with what most of us would think an unusual greeting, *"Consider it pure joy, my brothers and sisters, whenever you face trials of many kinds, because you know that the testing of your faith produces perseverance. Let perseverance finish its work so that you may be mature and complete, not lacking anything."*

Knowing what they were going through, James wanted to begin by helping them understand spiritual maturity is one of the biggest reasons God allows our faith to be tested. God wants us to grow. He wants us to be spiritually mature believers!

In the Kingdom of God, maturity and success are related. Success is measured by our ability to be spiritually mature in handling the testing of our faith. Tests of faith come in a variety of ways at different times in our lives. Tests mold us and help us grow into spiritually mature, well-balanced individuals. Spiritual maturity is measured by our capacity to respond effectively – in a way that brings God glory – even when we experience tragedy and chaos.

The Testing of Faith

How do you handle chaos? What do you do when suddenly everything collapses around you? How do you handle the unexpected, tragedy, difficulties, issues? Our actions in that moment reveal how spiritually mature we truly are.

We can tell a person's spiritual maturity level by how they handle pressure, tragedy, or difficulties in their lives. In other words, we never truly know a person until we observe their behavior under stress.

Pressure not only reveals our spiritual maturity level; it also reveals our character. Can we rise to the occasion of the unexpected, the chaotic, even the tragic? Does our faith stand firm and grow under the tests of life? Or does our world have to remain neat, orderly, and unruffled in order for us to deal with life?

The number one problem in our churches, communities, and our country is spiritual immaturity. God is looking for mature men and women to carry on His work and establish His kingdom, but often what He finds instead of spiritual mature men and women are little children who can't even get along with one another.

BELIEVE

The Testing of Faith

Now we see why James opens his letter with straight talk. He clearly says the reason God tests our faith is because He wants us to grow up, to be spiritually mature believers. The only way we can get there is by the testing of our faith. Let's dive in as James breaks down the details about the testing of our faith and how it helps us grow up God's way.

<u>The Testing of Faith Clarifies What Is Most Important</u>
In James 1:2, James writes, *"My brethren, count it all joy when you fall into various trials…"* He doesn't say "if" we fall into various trials, but "when" we fall into various trials. The message for us as believers is we should NOT be surprised when we encounter difficulties and challenges and our faith is tested by trials.

Jesus warned us first in John 16:33, when He said, *"I have told you these things, so that in me you may have peace. In this world you will have trouble. But take heart! I have overcome the world."*

The Testing of Faith

Paul cautioned us as well in Acts 14:22, saying, *"We must go through many hardships to enter the kingdom of God."*

Peter advised similarly in 1 Peter 4:12, telling us, *"Dear friends, do not be surprised at the fiery ordeal that has come on you to test you, as though something strange were happening to you."*

James, as the brother of Jesus and a prominent leader in the Church tells us plainly, it is not a matter of "if" but "when." The world "fall" doesn't mean we trip up into trials, but rather that we will encounter or come across trials in our path.

The NKJV says, *"fall into various trials."* The NIV says, *"face trials of many kinds."* The Message says, *"when tests and challenges come at you from all sides."* As believers, we know what it feels like! The point is these tests and trials are not all alike, but different and varied. The word picture James is painting here in the original Greek is akin to the picture of the various types of yarn a weaver uses to make a beautiful rug.

BELIEVE

I remember when my wife and I were traveling in Asia. We had been to Beijing and Shanghai and we were on the way to Hong Kong. There are artists in Asia who are known all over the world to be master weavers with yarn. In fact, their works are so detailed their pictures look like paintings though they are actually yarn. We had heard about it and our tour guide was going to take us there. We walked into this weaver's shop. We stood watching the weavers at work and honestly, at first I didn't understand the hype – how was this what I had heard described? I was seeing all the various colors of thread, all the knots, dangling yarn, and I was not impressed – until the tour guide came over and told me I was looking at the wrong side. When I stepped on the other side, I was awestruck and said, "Wow, this IS a beautiful picture!"

The point – often when we go through the testing of our faith, we are looking at the wrong side of the situation and we are thinking why does God have me going through this? Only God knows what He is weaving together and at the right time God will let you see the other side and understand what He has been weaving together is a beautiful tapestry. Only God knows the finished pattern. This is why we need to focus on what James tells us in verse 2, *"count it all joy."*

The Testing of Faith

The word which is translated as "count" is a financial term which means "to evaluate." More specifically it means "to evaluate your life in light of what is most important." James is saying we need to evaluate our lives in light of what is most important. In other words, the testing of our faith, the trials of life, serve to help us clarify and determine what is most important in our lives.

I have a dear, dear friend, who some years ago, was hesitant to step through a door God had opened for him. It was clearly God. Everyone could see God was all over it. My friend did not want to step through it because he was concerned about what people who did not understand God or our culture would say. He was concerned how it would look to them and what would they say. I told him that they didn't matter – he needed to do what God told him to do.

He hesitated, contemplated his career, his network, and the like. He did not step through the door God had opened for him. A few years later, he went through a major trial in his personal life. It made a lot of news in certain circles. I didn't even hear about it from him, but from someone who knew I knew him.

BELIEVE

They told me he was really struggling, so I ended up calling him once I found out what was going on. I told him, "Hey, I'm reaching out to you. I love you man. I heard what you're going through. How are you doing?"

He started, "You tried to tell me." I asked, "What are you talking about?"

He answered, "Remember a couple of years ago when I didn't want to do what God was calling me to do because I was so concerned with what others would think?"

I agreed, "Yes."

He went on, "I was doing some business with those individuals, and the moment I went through this trial, and tragedy in my life, they were the first ones to drop me. You know what I realize now – those relationships weren't about anything – what I realize now is I need to focus on what God called me to do and stop worrying about other people think!"

The test he went through helped him to clarify what was most important! It is exactly what the testing of our faith does!

The Testing of Faith

It is the reason Job in Job 23:10 says, *"But He knows the way that I take; When He has tested me, I shall come forth as gold."* When gold is refined, it goes through a purification process which burns off anything unneeded, burns off the impure, burns off anything that does not increase the value of the gold.

It is what a test of your faith does. When we go through tests of our faith, there are things which used to be a part of our lives that will burn off – ways of thinking, people we thought we needed, etc. God will burn it all off of us and we will learn what is truly valuable in life. It is not living a life for other people or bending our life to what they say or what they think. God will strip our lives of all that through the test!

It is why James tells us to *"count it all joy…"* We can have joy in the midst of the testing of our faith because the testing helps us key in on what matters most and what is most important in our lives! We can have joy even in the testing when we know what is most important – God is in our corner, our family is with us, our real friends are supporting us.

BELIEVE

The Testing of Faith Works for Us, Not Against Us and Helps Us Mature

In James 1:3 (NKJV), James writes, "...*knowing that the testing of your faith produces patience.*" The KJV translates it, "...knowing this, that the trying of your faith worketh patience." The word translated as "trying" or "testing" means "approval." It is another word picture used by James and it denotes a gold prospector. When someone is prospecting for gold and believe they've found it, they take a small sample of the gold to an assayer's office to be tested. The sample, because of the size, is not worth much, but the approval from the assayer is worth millions. Why? It assures the prospector that he in fact has a gold mine in his possession.

It's like when my wife is cooking and she asks me, "Taste this..." just to make sure the dish is seasoned well. She doesn't bring me the whole pot but only a little taste on a small spoon. If I give her the nod of approval, it indicates the whole pot is good.

When we go through trials and the testing of our faith, they work for us, in our favor.

The Testing of Faith

God is testing a small part of our life in order to determine if our faith is real. If we go through the trial and fall apart – God knows our faith is not real. If we go through the trial and still bless God with our head held high, praising Him and having the faith that on the other side we'll come out like pure gold – God knows our faith is good and genuine.

Peter explains the premise in 1 Peter 1:3-7:

Praise be to the God and Father of our Lord Jesus Christ! In his great mercy he has given us new birth into a living hope through the resurrection of Jesus Christ from the dead, and into an inheritance that can never perish, spoil, or fade. This inheritance is kept in heaven for you, who through faith are shielded by God's power until the coming of the salvation that is ready to be revealed in the last time. In all this you greatly rejoice, though now for a little while you may have had to suffer grief in all kinds of trials. These have come so that the proven genuineness of your faith—of greater worth than gold, which perishes even though refined by fire—may result in praise, glory and honor when Jesus Christ is revealed.

BELIEVE

Peter tells us God has laid up an inheritance for us and He has more for us but we will go through trials and the testing of our faith because the way we handle those prove our faith is genuine. The testing works for us letting us know the strength of our faith, but they also help us become spiritually mature. God wants to develop patience, endurance, and the ability to trust Him and keep going even when things are tough!

The word "patience" doesn't mean a passive acceptance of circumstances but rather **courageous perseverance in the face of suffering and difficulty**. The word is also translated as "endurance" or "perseverance" in other translations. The words are often used interchangeably in Scripture.

Real patience is not you hanging back, sitting around waiting on God, and doing nothing. Real patience means you are courageously persevering in the face of suffering and difficulty. Real patience says, "I know I don't see it yet but I know God is going to bring me through." Real patience declares, "You don't have to believe for me, I believe for myself." Real patience declares, "I am going to wait on the Lord because I know those who wait on the Lord, the Lord will renew their strength" (Isaiah 40:31).

The Testing of Faith

Here is the truth – spiritually immature people are always impatient. They are always asking, "God when are you going to do it?" They are the ones who come to church a week or two and then say, "God I did what you asked, when are you going to move?" They are the ones who declare, "I tried Jesus but…" when in truth it is God who "tried" them (remember – "the trying of your faith.") They are the first to walk away, the first to fall apart, not realizing God was working to develop their patience.

In Proverbs 24:10, in the Message translation, we find this truth, *"If you fall to pieces in a crisis, there wasn't much to you in the first place."* It is the reason impatience and unbelief go hand in hand.

Conversely spiritually mature people are patient and persistent. They don't take "no" for an answer when the Word says yes. It does not matter how long it takes. My grandmother used to say, "You can't make me doubt Him because I know too much about Him." Spiritually mature people will wait on the Lord—they know God will come through. Impatience and unbelief go hand in hand but faith and patience go together.

BELIEVE

God's Word urges us in Hebrews 6:12, "*We do not want you to become lazy, but to imitate those who through <u>faith and patience</u> inherit what has been promised.*" Faith and patience is what Abraham had to have to get to Isaac!

Later in Hebrews 10:36, we are encouraged similarly, "*You need to <u>persevere</u> so that when you have done the will of God, you will receive what he has promised.*"

Sometimes we do the will of God but when we don't see immediate results, we get frustrated and fail to persevere. We have to persevere – it is the faith and patience the writer of Hebrews encourages. It means we do what He says, and we know that while we might not see the results tomorrow – we will see the results so we continue to be faithful to what He called us to do. God does not lie, what He says is true. We do His will and we wait on the harvest, day after day, until we see the result – that is perseverance. We know we do not sow and harvest the same day or even the same week. We have to persevere so when we have done the will of God we will receive what He has promised.

The Testing of Faith

God wants us to be patient (to have courageous perseverance in the face of difficulty). Why? It is the key to every other blessing He has for us! When we, as believers, develop this kind of patience (courageous perseverance in the face of difficulty) then God can do even greater things through us because we are willing to wait on Him! If we don't develop this kind of patience, we will always try to get ahead of God, to make things happen on our own, and we will ultimately get into trouble.

Prior to the birth of Isaac, Abraham got ahead of God – married Hagar and brought great sorrow and chaos into his own home.

Moses got ahead of God, murdered a man, buried him in the sand, and then had to spend 40 years on the backside of a desert waiting for God.

Peter got ahead of God when they came to arrest Jesus. Peter cut off a man's ear and almost killed him.

BELIEVE

The only way God can develop this type of patience—courageous perseverance in the face of difficulty—in us is through tests and trials. We can't get it by reading a book, listening to a message, or even praying a prayer. The only way to get this kind of patience is to go through tests and trials.

Remember when the Israelites came to Jericho (Joshua 6). God told them to walk around the city for seven days and then on the seventh day to walk around the city seven times, blow the trumpets, and the walls would come down. It is an image of the patience and perseverance God wants to grow in us. The problem for many of us is we will walk around once or twice and get angry because the walls don't fall. We have to have the patience to keep walking (doing the will of God) because as we continue to do what God has called us to do, He will use us and the walls will ultimately come tumbling down! It comes through faith and patience – courageous perseverance in the face of difficulty.

The Testing of Faith

The Testing of Faith Determines If We Have Surrendered Our Will

In James 1:4, James continues, *"But let patience have its perfect work, that you may be perfect and complete, lacking nothing."* God's goal for our lives is spiritual maturity – that we "may be perfect and complete, lacking nothing."

Parents, consider this – how great a tragedy it would be if your babies remained babies for the rest of their lives?

Many believers do their best to run away from and avoid every test of their faith. The result – they never grow up but remain babies their whole lives! In spite of ourselves, God works to make sure we grow. How? God works for us, in us, and through us!

The working for us is what He did for us through His Son, Jesus Christ. He works in us – it is the work of sanctification – molding us to be more like Him. When He has worked for us and in us, then He can work through us.

BELIEVE

The challenge is – God cannot work in us without our consent. Giving our consent means surrendering our will. Sometimes this takes much longer than it needs to because we will not surrender our will – we will not die to self.

God spent 25 years working in Abraham before He could give him Isaac. God spent 13 years working in Joseph's life before He could put him on the throne of Egypt. God spent 80 years working in Moses' life before He could lead the nation of Israel for 40 years.

God working in us often takes a while. Why? The length of time it takes for God to work in us directly correlates to how long it takes us to surrender our will to Him.

We often miss a really big truth in the story of Abraham taking Isaac to the top of Mt. Moriah to sacrifice him in Genesis 22. The big truth we often miss is the fact that Isaac is not a baby. In fact, scholars believe he was between 16 and 25 years old.

The Testing of Faith

This means Isaac had to willingly lay down his life on that altar.

A big truth in the death of our Savior is that no one took his life, He voluntarily laid His life down for us (John 10:18). It is with this understanding that Paul writes in Romans 12:1, *"Therefore, I urge you, brothers and sisters, in view of God's mercy, to offer your bodies as a living sacrifice, holy and pleasing to God—this is your true and proper worship."*

Paul is telling us to lay down our lives in light of all God has done for us. He desires that we surrender our will! Here is the problem, many of us will lay down on the altar as long as it is comfortable, but the moment a test of faith comes, we jump up off the altar.

Everything about our faith tells us that after death there is a resurrection. Everything about our faith testifies that dying is not the end. God is going to do more on the other side but we have to die first.

BELIEVE

There is a resurrection after death. Think about it – we celebrate it and sing about the power of the resurrection, but the fact is in order to experience it we have to die first. We want the resurrection, we want the triumph, we want the victory…but we don't want to die first. We don't want to lay on the altar and surrender our will and yet that is exactly what surrendering our will is all about!

James says so we "may be perfect and complete, lacking nothing." When we surrender our will, it feels like we are giving up everything, but no, we are positioning ourselves to get everything. James reiterates, "lacking nothing." When we try to work it out on our own, we are always "lacking something." The moment we lay it down, God says, "Now I can give you everything."

Surrendering our will is dying to what we want so what God wants for us can happen. A spiritually mature person will lay it all down on the altar and when the test of faith comes, they don't jump up, they don't argue – they accept His will and they joyfully obey His will.

The Testing of Faith

Earlier, I told you part of my faith story, how I was sitting in King Chapel at Morehouse College and I confessed how I wasn't living by faith, how I surrendered, and God took me to some incredible places.

What I did not share was the hardest part of it all was to let go of my will and to trust what God had for me was far better than anything I could ever try to create for myself. It was truly a test of faith, in fact the challenge of surrendering my will was the test, behind the test.

Whatever you are going through – finances, marriage, career – yes, it is a test. But the test behind the test is "Will you trust that what God has for you is better than anything you could ever attempt to create on your own?"

The biggest challenge I had was holding on so tightly to what I wanted, the way I wanted it, when I wanted it. God kept telling me to "let it go" as He sent me test after test after test.

BELIEVE

I kept holding on to it and each test was designed to get me to lay it all down. Finally, I stopped holding on to my will and I let go. As soon as I got out of His way God gave me so much more! As soon as I got out of the way God said, "Now I can do what I want to do." What God has done is better than anything I could have tried to create.

Will you trust God, get on the altar, and lay it all down, surrendering your will so He can work?

Reflection

How do you handle chaos? What do you do when
suddenly everything collapses around you?
How do you handle the unexpected, tragedy,
difficulties, issues? Can you rise to the occasion
of the unexpected, the chaotic, even the tragic?
Does your faith stand firm and grow under the
tests of life? Or does your world have to remain
neat, orderly, and unruffled in order for you to
deal with life?

Think of your most recent trials/tests. How have
those tests/trials helped you hone in on what
was truly important in your life?

Did those trials help you mature in your faith,
build patience, become more resilient, endure?
How?

We have all gotten ahead of God at some time.
Recall a time you got ahead of God – how did
you see God work to resolve the situation?

Will you trust that what God has for you is
better than anything you could ever attempt to
create on your own? Will you surrender?

Chapter 7
God's Faith Building Process

"He called down famine on the land and destroyed all their supplies of food; and he sent a man before them—Joseph, sold as a slave. They bruised his feet with shackles, his neck was put in irons, till what he foretold came to pass, till the word of the Lord proved him true." ~Psalm 105:16-19

In this chapter we will continue to uncover the truths of genuine Biblical faith and more importantly discover one of the most important factors we must understand in order to live by faith – **God's Faith Building Process**.

In Psalm 105:16-19, we read, *"**He** called down famine on the land and destroyed all their supplies of food; and **He** sent a man before them—Joseph, sold as a slave. They bruised his feet with shackles, his neck was put in irons, till what **he** foretold came to pass, till the word of the Lord proved him true."*

BELIEVE

The Word says, *"He called down famine…"* Who is He? God *"called down famine…"* The Word says, *"He sent a man before them…"* Who is He? God *"sent a man before them…"* The Word says, *"…until what He foretold came to pass."* Who is He? *"…Until what God foretold came to pass till the word of the Lord proved him true."*

We are starting in Psalm 105 as we explore God's Faith Building Process because these verses are extremely important in helping us understand a new perspective about the familiar story of Joseph. Often when we think of the story of Joseph, we think about it from Genesis as if Joseph is living it in real time. We know Joseph had a dream – a vision from God. Mistakenly and prematurely, Joseph shared the dream with his brothers. In anger and jealously, they dropped him into a pit, sold him into slavery, and told their father Joseph was dead.

We know as a slave, he was a servant in Potiphar's house. There he tried to do the right thing even when Potiphar's wife makes sexual advances toward him. He does not engage so she lies about the encounter, which leads to him being wrongfully imprisoned.

God's Faith Building Process

We also know he languished in prison for many years. When we read the story from that perspective we see it with great sympathy, with great anger. If we put ourselves in Joseph's shoes, we can feel the agony in the story and disbelief over his brothers mistreatment of him, Potiphar's wife's lies, and even those he helped in prison who forgot him.

Psalm 105 helps us to understand there is a completely different perspective. Often we only think about the narrative from the vantage point of Joseph but Psalm 105 serves to remind us of the other vantage point – God's. God orchestrated it all. God called down the famine on the land, God was the one who destroyed all their supplies in order to get people to Egypt. God was the one who got Joseph there. It is interesting because when you read Psalm 105, you see it from God's perspective. God had been orchestrating it all because there was a process God wanted Joseph to walk through to get him where He needed him to be.

BELIEVE

There was nothing random or haphazard about anything Joseph went through. It may have felt that way from Joseph's perspective but from God's perspective it was all intentional. Every step – the pit, Potiphar's house, prison, and ultimately the palace, was intentional as God was building Joseph's faith for where He was ultimately taking him. God always has a process.

Many years ago, when my children were small, before we became vegan, my wife and I were pescatarians. While we were on a family vacation in Mexico, the first night there we decided to go into town to eat. We headed into town and found this really cool restaurant advertising this incredible deal on a lobster dinner. We headed inside to get the lobster deal.

The problem was I had never had Caribbean lobster before – the only lobster I knew was New England lobster. When the Caribbean lobster was brought out, I was freaking out, "Man, I can't eat this – there is something wrong with this lobster!"

God's Faith Building Process

The waiter tried to calm me. I kept on, "No, no, no, send it back, I'm not eating this!" I continued leaning over to my brother-in-law, "Man, they are trying to get over on us, we are in Mexico, we need to be more wise." I kept on and on, literally freaking out. Everyone at the table went silent and it was then I knew something was wrong but I was still freaking out!

The manager of the restaurant came over and said, "Sir, these are Caribbean lobsters, they don't have the claws like the lobsters in Maine." He went on to explain, "You are used to the New England lobsters but this is a Caribbean lobster. It is a good lobster, there is nothing wrong with it – it is not deformed."

I felt about an inch tall. Why? Because I just didn't know!

I was freaking out over lobsters, but often many of us freak out over life because we just don't know. We often think something is the wrong or a calamity has happened or God has forgotten us, when in reality it is simply the process God is taking us through to build our faith.

BELIEVE

I'm often asked, "Why is this happening to me? I don't understand it! Did I miss God? Did He forget about me? I'm doing everything I'm supposed to be doing." When we don't understand God's Faith Building Process, we worry and can get easily discouraged. We may become resentful. We may become fearful about the future. We may become depressed and most of all we cannot cooperate with what God is doing.

On the other hand, when we understand God's Faith Building Process we can cooperate with what God is doing to bring about His plan – His best for us. It is the same process that God takes every believer through (often over and over and over again). In Hebrews 11, the Hall of Fame of Faith, we read, "By faith, Noah…by faith, Moses…by faith, Rahab…" and on through all of those individuals who all went through God's Faith Building Process.

When we understand it, then we can rightly understand where we are and we can say, "Oh, I'm in stage four right now" or "stage six" or "stage two."

God's Faith Building Process

When we understand God's Faith Building Process, we don't get discouraged, we don't fall apart when we get to certain stages in the process because we understand those stages. We are able to recognize what God is doing though those stages when times seem tough.

What is God's Faith Building Process?

In this chapter, we will examine God's Faith Building Process in steps/stages.

Step 1 – The Dream

God always starts with a dream. Our faith makes the dream possible. In Genesis 15:5-6, we see God deliver the dream to Abram, *"He took him outside and said, 'Look up at the sky and count the stars—if indeed you can count them.' Then he said to him, 'So shall your offspring be.' Abram believed the Lord, and he credited it to him as righteousness."* Abraham did not have children at this point but what makes him righteous was that He believed God. Because he believed God, then by faith he is able to dream about the family to come.

BELIEVE

For example, we read in the Word of God – *"and He will supply all of your needs according to His riches in glory"* (Philippians 4:19) and we believe it, we are able to start dreaming. We don't need to live in a place of fear or panic or lack because God promised and the promise is what unlocks the dream.

When we recognize and believe, "There is no good thing that God will withhold from those who walk uprightly," (Psalm 84:11) the belief is what unlocks the dream.

Jesus says, *"All things are possible to those who believe"* (Mark 9:23) – it is the belief that unlocks the dream and we can really tap into all that God can do! We see and believe, "God can use us to do this, God can do that," and we begin to dream! Faith is the key to the dream but just like for Abraham, our dream begins in the Word of God.

In Hebrews 11:1, the writer tells us, *"Now faith is the substance of things hoped for, the evidence of things not seen,"* we know that which is hoped for, that which is not seen, is where the dream is and faith makes it possible.

God's Faith Building Process

It is the way God did it with every major individual in the Bible. Earlier we saw in Mark 9:23, *"All things are possible to him who believes"* and the Bible provides many examples of this truth.

God spoke a Word to Noah and Noah believed – the dream was birthed and Noah began building the ark for the coming deluge. God spoke a Word to Joseph, Joseph believed and He began to dream of becoming a leader who would save his people. God gave a Word to Nehemiah, Nehemiah believed, and the dream of restoring the walls around the city of Jerusalem began. God gave a Word to David, David began to trust and believe the dream of building a temple for the Lord. Nothing happens until we begin to believe the Word and start dreaming.

His Faith Building Process always begins with the dream. It is the reason the Apostle Paul is trying to get the Church at Ephesus to understand just how big God is and why we are supposed to believe God for big things.

BELIEVE

In Ephesians 3:20, we find the promise, *"Now to Him who is able to do exceedingly abundantly above all that we ask or think, according to the power that works in us."* Paul is telling the members of the Church at Ephesus, "You're thinking to small! If you understand how big God is and if you trust Him you need to start dreaming for your life, dreaming for your family, and dreaming for your future. The dream is always step one of God's Faith Building Process.

Step 2 – Decision

After the dream comes step two – the decision – the point in which we begin to do something about our dream. Nothing will happen by way of faith until we make the decision to act on God's Word in faith. We've got to make the decision and declare, "I'm going for it!" Breakthrough has nothing to do with how much of the Word we know, it has everything to do with how much Word we do!

Remember, in Hebrews 4:2, *"For indeed the gospel was preached to us as well as to them; but the word which they heard did not profit them, not being mixed with faith in those who heard it."*

God's Faith Building Process

When we get the dream we have to have the faith to do something with it! The Word of faith is available to everyone, but the fruit of it will only manifest in the lives of people who decide to act on it.

James testifies to this truth, *"Thus also faith by itself, if it does not have works is dead" (James 2:17). We earlier defined "works" as* "corresponding acts of obedience." We get the Word and God expects us to obey it. Why? Faith is a verb. It is active, not passive. Faith is what you do. Decision making is, in itself, a faith building activity.

God comes to Abraham in Genesis 12:1-2, *"The Lord had said to Abram, 'Go from your country, your people and your father's household to the land I will show you. I will make you into a great nation, and I will bless you; I will make your name great, and you will be a blessing.'"*

God gives the Word – He will make Abraham a great nation but Abraham has to leave his country, his family, everything he knows. He has a decision to make and it is in that decision that his faith begins to build.

BELIEVE

God shows up in a burning bush, after Moses has spent forty years on the backside of a Midianite desert. In Exodus 3:9-10, God tells Moses, *"And now the cry of the Israelites has reached me, and I have seen the way the Egyptians are oppressing them. So now, go. I am sending you to Pharaoh to bring my people the Israelites out of Egypt."* God is sending him back to the very place he fled forty years earlier because he murdered a man and buried him in the sand, and as a result the Pharoah was looking for him in order to kill him. God tells him to go to the Pharoah and say, "Let my people go."

Moses has a decision to make.

Saul is on the Damascus Road heading to persecute more Christians. God shows up as a light from heaven and blinds Saul before speaking to him in Acts 9:4-6, *"Saul, Saul, why do you persecute me?"*
'Who are you, Lord?' Saul asked.
'I am Jesus, whom you are persecuting,' he replied. 'Now get up and go into the city, and you will be told what you must do.'

God's Faith Building Process

Saul, who we also know as Paul, has a decision to make.

And often, when God gives us that first Word, we won't hear anything else from Him until we decide to act on His Word. God speaks to Abraham in Genesis 12, but Abraham doesn't hear from God again until Genesis 15 after Abraham acts on the Word from the Lord. If he had decided to do nothing, God would have said, "Well, there is nothing else for me to say."

God didn't speak again to Moses after the burning bush until Moses gets moving toward what God had told him to do.

During this step, we have a decision to make. We won't experience anything else from God until after we make the decision. During this phase—in decision making— we must do two things:

1. **We must invest.**
   a. Our Time
   b. Our Money
   c. Our Reputation
   d. Our Energy

BELIEVE

Our investment is the point in which we lay it all on the line, the place we take the plunge. It is where we say, "God, You told me to do this and I'm going to go for it!" We can't go for it and not make an investment at the same time.

2. We have to let go of security

We cannot move in faith toward the future and hold on to the past at the same time. In order to move forward in faith and make the decision to trust God we have to let go of something!

For Abraham: God said, *"I'm going to make you the father of a great nation."* In order to move forward in faith, he had to leave his home and his family for an unknown destination.

For Joshua: God tells Joshua to lead the nation of Israel into the Promised Land, but in order to move forward in faith, he has to let go of all he had known as Moses' protégé for the last forty years!

For Nehemiah: Nehemiah had to let go of a comfortable and secure job as the cupbearer to the king in order to move forward in faith and rebuild the walls around Jerusalem.

God's Faith Building Process

In other words, if we really want to walk on water, we've got to get out of the boat.

Letting go of security is best exemplified in the work of trapeze artists. They swing out on bars attached to ropes and then let go, grabbing another set of similar bars and swinging to the other side. The bars are placed far enough apart so they cannot hang on to the first and grab the other at the same time. At some point they have to let go of the first bar to grab on to the other one which means for a split second they are holding on to neither. They are suspended in mid-air for that split second with nothing to hold on to!

It is exactly what living by faith feels like – we are letting go of the first bar to get to the next bar to which God is leading us. Have you ever been there in your career – you're leaving one job for another and there is nothing to support you in between?

You're up there – 180 feet above – no net below and nothing on which to hold.

BELIEVE

What happens when we try to hold on to our past –
that which makes us comfortable? If you don't let go and
grab the next thing God has provided and desires for
you, you swing back. The problem is you don't swing all
the way back, instead you simply swing back and forth
as the momentum slows and you go slower and slower
until you stop – hanging there with only one way out –
down. The only way to get another opportunity is to go
down and climb back up to start over.

Step 3 – Delay

Step one – God gives us a dream. Faith allows us to
dream.
Step two – we have to make a decision whether or not to
go for it.
Step three is a delay. The promise of God does not
happen immediately. There is always a delay, a waiting
period, a time lapse.

In Habakkuk 2:2, the Lord says, "...*Write down the
revelation and make it plain on tablets so that a herald
may run with it.*"

God's Faith Building Process

In the next verse, God goes on, *"For the revelation awaits an appointed time; it speaks of the end and will not prove false. Though it linger, wait for it; it will certainly come and will not delay."* God says, "Write it…Get ready to run with it…But it's not going to happen right away." It's worth repeating as it speaks of *"an end that will not prove false, though it linger, wait for it, for it certainly will come and it will not delay."*

In step three, at this stage, we start asking, "When, Lord? When are You going to do it…?" Sometimes, we even get mad with God, "God, I heard the Word, I've done what You asked, I have the dream, I've stepped out," because He hasn't done it as fast as we want Him to do it. "When are you going to do it God?"

Every believer in history has gone to the "University of Learning to Wait" and for many us we are still awaiting our degree. Some of us are trying to cut class, and God is saying, "No, you have to past this test."

Noah waited 120 years from the time he started building the ark until it began to rain.

BELIEVE

Abraham waited 25 years for Isaac, the son of the promise.

After telling Moses he would lead His people out of 400 years of slavery, God had Moses wait in the desert 40 years.

Joseph waited 13 years from the time he had the dream and found himself in the pit to the day he found himself in the palace.

David waited 15 years after being anointed king by Samuel to actually be crowned King of Israel.

We will go through waiting periods. Even Jesus waited for 30 years before beginning His public ministry and becoming the world's Messiah.

Why does God call us to wait? What He is doing in us is way more important than where He is trying to bring us. The worst thing God could do is promote us to a place we are not ready to handle or open a door we are not ready to step through.

God's Faith Building Process

Waiting is part of the process. God is working in us and teaching us to trust Him and understand His timing is perfect. He is developing us in the waiting.

Let's backtrack a minute to when we discussed the testing of faith. When the Bible talks about faith and patience – patience doesn't mean that we sit down and wait. Patience means "courageous perseverance in the face of difficulty." It means we remain actively busy while we wait on God to move.

The Bible often speaks of waiting on the Lord as in Isaiah 40:31, "...*but those who hope in the Lord will renew their strength. They will soar on wings like eagles; they will run and not grow weary, they will walk and not be faint.*" Waiting doesn't mean we are crossing our arms, sitting back, and doing nothing. This verse is describing patience, being actively engaged, and working because we know God is going to come through.

This became clear to me when I was in graduate school. I was working at a fine dining restaurant atop the Hyatt Regency in downtown Atlanta.

BELIEVE

I worked there as a bartender and waiter. As I mixed
drinks for those who came to the bar, they didn't pay
up front. They placed their order for cocktails, and I
made the cocktails trusting that when the bill came they
would pay. The same premise was true when I waited
tables. They ordered first, I placed the orders with the
sous chef, their meals were prepared, I served the food at
the table. All the time I'm working while I'm waiting for
them to pay. They ate their meals, I offered dessert. After
all of that, I brought the bill. I did all the work trusting
that when the bill came to be paid, they would pay it.

It is the same approach God is asking for from us – He
is saying, "Don't check out and think I have forgotten
you – work while you wait – because when "the bill
comes due, I will pay it. Check My record, I've never
missed a payment."

Our waiting means God is working and we are to be
actively engaged in that process. We can do it when we
understand the difference between "No" and "Not yet."

God's Faith Building Process

So often, we freak out because we think God is saying, "No," when He is really saying, "Not yet." We assume the delay is a denial and God says, "No, I'm still going to keep My Word, I'm still going to do what I have promised You I would do, but not yet.'"

There were so many times in my life where I was bumping up against a wall thinking I was supposed to lead this church here, or be there, and God kept closing doors, and I did get upset with God because no one had taught me God's Faith Building Process. Now, looking back on it, I recognize and I thank God for every one of the closed doors because they were leading me to His correct timing and the place He needed me to be.

God may delay but He never destroys His purpose because a delay is not a denial. A delay never destroys God's purpose in your life.

BELIEVE

Step 4 – Difficulty

Step one is the dream. Step two is the decision. Step three is delay. Step four is difficulty. Not only do we get to wait, we get to have other problems while we wait. There are two primary types of problems – circumstances and critics – and we can count on them both. When we begin to move in faith, there will always be circumstances which get in our way and critics who, well, criticize.

My wife and I recently had the opportunity to go back to Ft. Lauderdale, Florida after traveling internationally for two weeks. For 10 days, we helped lead a group of 92 people through the footsteps of Paul and traced his journey in Acts 17-19. We went through Thessalonica, Ephesus, Corinth, Berea, and Athens.

When the tour was complete, my wife and I flew to Ft. Lauderdale which is where we lived before God brought us to Birmingham. We went there because the Pastor at the church I served for four years was retiring. He had served there for 38 years, and he had invited me to speak as part of his retirement celebration.

God's Faith Building Process

We arrived late on Friday, attended a retirement brunch on Saturday. After the brunch, my wife said, "Let's drive around and see our old neighborhoods and our first home together." We went around, seeing it all and reminiscing, and thanking God for Birmingham and for the last 18 years of The Worship Center.

Why? Right before God moved us to Birmingham, my wife had earned her doctoral degree (yes, before me). She had gotten her dream job – a professor at a university. She was on staff at St. Thomas University and she was working toward tenure. Then, I got the call to go to Birmingham. She had to go to her colleagues and tell them, "This is my dream job, but I'm going to have to resign. My husband and I are moving to Birmingham."

They clowned her, everyone at the university said, "You got your dream job and you are going to leave it to follow a preacher to Birmingham." They got nasty and really cruel.

It didn't stop there, preachers I knew around the country called me as asked, "Are you really moving to Birmingham to do ministry? God is not doing anything new in Birmingham.

BELIEVE

There is no fresh new faith movement in Birmingham. It would make sense if you were going to Dallas or Atlanta, or another major city, but Birmingham!"

We had all kinds of critics, but while we were riding around in Ft. Lauderdale, we were thanking God for what He had done, for The Worship Center, for Birmingham. We thanked Him for not leaving us in Ft. Lauderdale.

Why? Because we will have critics! In fact, critics and circumstances are proof in many ways that we are moving in faith. If we don't have any circumstances or critics coming against us, we may want to check if we are in fact in the will of God. All through scripture, whenever the people of God were getting ready to move in faith – there were always critics, there were always circumstances.

Moses had difficulty, after difficulty, after difficulty. He led the children of Israel out of the certainty of slavery in Egypt into the uncertain future of a journey across the desert to the Promised Land.

God's Faith Building Process

He experienced one problem after another. First they had no water. Next they had no food. Everyone became a bunch of complainers. Then came the poisonous snakes that bit many people. They had one problem after another even though they were doing what God wanted – traveling to the Promised Land.

David was anointed king but he went back to the pasture. Later he began working for Saul, then Saul was trying to kill him and he spent the next several years being hunted by Saul and forced to hide in caves though he had done nothing wrong. He was in the will of God, but he faced problem after problem after problem.

Joseph had a dream of becoming a ruler and then he was sold into slavery and falsely accused of rape. He languished in prison with no one even knowing he was there. He asked those he helped in prison to help him but they forgot. He watched as difficulties piled on top of delays.

Imagine the critics Noah had – building an ark for 120 years because of a coming flood though there had never before been any rain.

BELIEVE

They were probably saying things like "I knew there was something wrong with Noah when he was born... somebody dropped him or he bumped his head...Noah has lost it...we need to pray for him...bless his heart."

We will have circumstances, we will have critics, we will have all kinds of problems every day on our journey of faith.

The Bible tells us when Moses died, Joshua was appointed the leader. Moses had led the people across the desert but Joshua was the one who led them into the promised land. It almost seems as if Joshua had the easier part, but did he? Joshua leads them into the Promised Land, and the very next verses read, "Now there were giants in the land" (Numbers 13:28).

Even in the Promised Land, problems remained because God was working on their character and faith. Even in our promised land, as we face the challenges, God is growing us, molding and shaping us to give us the opportunity to know our faith is real.

God's Faith Building Process

Why does God allow these difficulties during the delays? In 1 Peter 1:6-7, Peter explains, *"At present you may be temporarily harassed by all kinds of trials. This is no accident. It happens to prove your faith which is infinitely more valuable than gold."*

If we didn't have circumstances and critics, we would not need faith. If everything was easy, we would not need faith. The challenge of believing beyond what is currently in front of us – that is what faith is!

Step 5 – Dead End

Step one – through faith we begin to dream. Step two – decision making – are we going to trust God. Step three brings delay. Step four sees difficulty. Even in the Promised Land, the Israelites faced difficulties and delays, and so did the many heroes of our faith.

Then comes step five, when the difficulties become so bad, we come to our limit. We've tried everything, and exhausted all our options and we come to a dead end.

BELIEVE

In these instances, the situation deteriorates from difficult to impossible. All appears hopeless, with no alternative remaining and no way out. When we get to this stage, rather than despair, we should offer ourselves congratulations. Every believer goes through it. The Apostle Paul described it this way in 2 Corinthians 1:8-9, *"At that time we were completely overwhelmed. The burden was more than we could bear. In fact, we told ourselves that this was the end. <u>Yet now we believe that we had this sense of impending disaster so that we might learn to trust not in ourselves but in God who can raise the dead."</u>*

Jesus went to the cross, gave up His life, and was raised from the dead not only to be our atoning sacrifice. Yes, He does that, the blood still has its power, without the shedding of blood there would be no remission of sins.

All true, the cross, the sacrifice, the resurrection... but this also helps us understand if God can raise the dead physically, then He can raise the dead emotionally. If God can resurrect the dead physically, then He can resurrect a dead marriage. If He can resurrect Jesus physically, He can resuscitate a dead career. He can resolve a health problem.

God's Faith Building Process

If God can raise the dead, He can do anything! It is a huge part of the hope we have as believers.

We have to see that God performs miracles and when it appears there is no other way. Isn't it interesting, when Lazarus is sick, they send for Jesus saying, *"Lazarus, whom You love is sick,"* (John 11:3) but Jesus simply says, *"His sickness is not unto death"* (John 11:4) and then stays where He was for several days? Why? If He had come when Lazarus was sick it would have only been a "nice" healing. Instead, He waited until Lazarus died, then He showed up, days later, and said, *"Show Me where you laid him"* (John 11:34). Why? When the situation gets to the place it looks humanly impossible, that is the time God steps in and works the way only He can work!

Remember what Jesus told us in Matthew 5:3 (MSG), *"You're blessed when you're at the end of your rope. With less of you there is more of God and his rule."* God is saying, "I have to get you to the end of yourself because if I intervene and you have not come to the end of yourself, you will try to take credit for it, you will try to say it was your spouse, significant other, or friend who helped you out or hooked you up.

BELIEVE

No, no, I will get all the glory. Let it get to a dead end and I will come in and turn it around, because then all you will be able to say is God did that!"

It is the reason it took all that time for Abraham and Sarah to have a baby. When Abraham was 75, God promises in Genesis 17:4, *"You will be the father of many nations."* Twenty-five years later, when Abraham is 100 years old, he and Sarah are still waiting to have a baby. God wanted Abraham to get good and "dead." He wanted Abraham to look at himself and say, "There is no way." God wanted Abraham to look at his wife, Sarah, and say, "Double no way!" God then said, "Now I'm going to do it." Then Sarah got pregnant and had a baby. When the baby was born, they named him Isaac, which means, "God laughs." They were saying, "God we didn't even think You were going to be able to do this, but clearly You got the last laugh!"

Some of us right now are thinking, just like Abraham and Sarah did, "There is no way, there is no way that this is even possible."

God's Faith Building Process

But we need to know God is going to get the last laugh! God is not done, but when He is, we will look back and say, "God, You are amazing, You are awesome, what You have done in my life is indescribable." In heaven, God will be laughing, "So you thought I was done? I'm not done, I am just getting started."

God often allows problems to become impossibilities on purpose because it is then that God begins to do His best work. When we get to this stage, we start asking, "What's going on, God? Did I miss your will? Your plan? Have I missed your vision? Is it really something I thought up? Is there sin in my life? Lord, if there is anything in me that I have done that is preventing you from getting all the glory from my life, I just want you to remove it right now." It is here we are at the end of ourselves, we have tried everything, and we are now to the point of "God if I am messing this thing up – deal with me!"

It is a common theme in the Bible – this Faith Building Process of God's – but one of the best examples comes in the Exodus narrative.

BELIEVE

In Exodus 14, Moses had finally led the Israelites out of Egypt where they had been slaves for 400 years. After the 10 horrific plagues, Pharoah told Moses and the Israelites, *"Get out of here! Good riddance!"* and they took off! God even blesses them as they leave making the Egyptians "favorable disposed" to them and they give the Israelites gold and silver and jewelry. They come out blessed – that is how great God is! God never just does what He promises, He does it better than we can ever image.

A few days later, Pharaoh changes his mind, realizing he has just given away his labor force, and starts coming after them. In the dramatic conclusion, the Israelites have reached the Red Sea, mountains at their sides. Behind them is their enemy, Pharoah and the Egyptian army in hot pursuit, ready to kill them. There is no way to escape. What do the Israelites do? They start freaking out – "What is going on God?" – because they did not understand God's Faith Building Process.

Let's read the account in Exodus 14:9-14 of what happened by the Red Sea that day:

God's Faith Building Process

"The Egyptians—all Pharaoh's horses and chariots, horsemen and troops—pursued the Israelites and overtook them as they camped by the sea near Pi Hahiroth, opposite <u>Baal Zephon</u>.

As Pharaoh approached, the Israelites looked up, and there were the Egyptians, marching after them. They were terrified and cried out to the Lord. They said to Moses, 'Was it because there were no graves in Egypt that you brought us to the desert to die? What have you done to us by bringing us out of Egypt? Didn't we say to you in Egypt, 'Leave us alone; let us serve the Egyptians'? It would have been better for us to serve the Egyptians than to die in the desert!'

[A Bonus Point: Don't ever allow the problems in your present to make you hold on to a dysfunctional past – a place you should have never been in the first place.]

*Moses answered the people, 'Do not be afraid. Stand firm and you will see the deliverance the Lord will bring you today. The Egyptians you see today you will never see again. **The Lord will fight for you; you need only to be still.**'*

BELIEVE

Some of us are struggling right now. We are in a tight place and we are struggling. We may know, *"Be still and know that I am God, "* (Psalm 46:10) but we are having a hard time being still. All we can see are the problems, the challenges, which seem insurmountable. How can we be still?

How could the Israelites be still? The place they camped and were hemmed in was a place called Baal-Zephon which just so happens to mean "God's hidden treasure." It means that in the jam, in the tight spot, in the struggle, is God's hidden treasure.

Do you see it? We can be still and know that God is going to fight for you, God is going to bring you out of what appears to be a dead end because like the Israelites, we are exactly where God wanted us to be. God knows where we are and He has our number. He knows every hair on our head. He put us in our dead end on purpose because that is the place of God's hidden treasure.

God's Faith Building Process

Step 6 – Deliverance

We start with the dream, we go to step two – the decision. We then go to stage three which is delay and then from delay, stage four which is difficulty. Before things get better, they get worse as we go from difficulty to step five – a dead end. How do we handle the dead ends?

The dead ends bring us to step six – deliverance. At the end, God always comes through, God always shows up and delivers. God does a miracle after miracle, after miracle. God provides a solution. Here's how it happens.

In Moses' case, God splits the Red Sea.

In Abraham's case, he and Sarah miraculously give birth a child.

In Joseph's case, he goes from the pit to Potiphar's house, to prison, to the palace, becoming the second in command in Egypt.

In Nehemiah's case, the walls are rebuilt in record time – 52 days.

BELIEVE

In David's case, he becomes the second King of Israel.

In the disciples' case, they thought Jesus's crucifixion was the end, but three days later, Jesus was resurrected from the dead.

God specializes in turning crucifixions into resurrections. He loves to transform dead ends into deliverance. Why? When He does, He gets all the credit and the glory, and we get His best for us!

Paul affirms the truth in 2 Corinthians 1:8-10:

We do not want you to be uninformed, brothers and sisters, about the troubles we experienced in the province of Asia. We were under great pressure, far beyond our ability to endure, so that we despaired of life itself. Indeed, we felt we had received the sentence of death. But this happened that we might not rely on ourselves but on God, who raises the dead. He has delivered us from such a deadly peril, and he will deliver us again. On him we have set our hope that he will continue to deliver us.

God's Faith Building Process

Paul tells us how to handle a dead end. We must move from worry to expectation. We know because of God's track record, because He has delivered before. He specializes in turning dead ends into deliverance - and we have to learn how to thank Him in advance for the deliverance that is to come. Paul testifies that they thought it was over, but he remembered that God had delivered them before and he knew God would deliver them in the future, so he knew God was delivering them even in that present moment. That is how we handle dead ends, we set our expectations on what we know God is going to do.

The best response to our dead end is to expect God to act – to thank Him in advance before He ever does it.

What are you expecting God to do in your life? If we answer that we aren't expecting Him to do anything, that is NOT faith. Faith IS after standing on the Word, living according to the Word, releasing our faith and speaking the Word, we have to start thanking God even before it happens. As we pray we need to be thanking Him in advance even before the deliverance comes. We can't wait until we get it, Faith IS "God I just want to thank you now" before we even see it.

BELIEVE

We need to thank God for the things we are still waiting for Him to do – from the dead end to deliverance.

Faith IS "God I know You are going to do it. You have never let me down and I just want to thank You now before the battle is over."

The author of 2 Chronicles 20:2,12,22-25, attests to this final stage of faith:

"Some people came and told Jehoshaphat, 'A vast army is coming against you from Edom, from the other side of the Dead Sea. It is already in Hazezon Tamar' (that is, En Gedi)...

Jehoshaphat gets the Word – He is at a dead end. This army is coming, in fact, already on the way. You don't have time to get ready.

Our God, will you not judge them? For we have no power to face this vast army that is attacking us. We do not know what to do, but our eyes are on you...'

God's Faith Building Process

We don't know what to do, but our eyes are on You…
we don't have to have the answer, we just have to keep
our eyes on God.

In verses 20-21, God tells them to put Judah out in
front and march into battle giving Me (God) praise and
thanks IN ADVANCE. Then,

> *As they began to sing and praise, the Lord set*
> *ambushes against the men of Ammon and Moab*
> *and Mount Seir who were invading Judah, and*
> *they were defeated.*

Do you see how powerful thanks and praise is? While
they were praising – God was already fighting their
battles.

> *The Ammonites and Moabites rose up against the*
> *men from Mount Seir to destroy and annihilate*
> *them. After they finished slaughtering the men*
> *from Seir, they helped to destroy one another.*

God took the enemy, and through the praise and thanks
of His people, sent the enemy into confusion. The
enemies that were coming against them started fighting
each other. We cannot let anyone tell us our praise is not
powerful.

BELIEVE

We cannot let ourselves believe our thanksgiving is not powerful. Start giving Him praise right now and watch for His deliverance.

> *When the men of Judah came to the place that overlooks the desert and looked toward the vast army, they saw only dead bodies lying on the ground; no one had escaped. So Jehoshaphat and his men went to carry off their plunder, and they found among them a great amount of equipment and clothing and also articles of value—more than they could take away. There was so much plunder that it took three days to collect it."*

They thought they were going to battle but God was setting it up to bless them. They carried off such a great amount – clothing, equipment, and other items of value – more than they could carry in one day. It took three days – Father, Son, and Holy Spirit – death, burial, and resurrection.

If we pray about it, if we trust Him, if we believe, God says, "Learn how to thank and praise Me in advance." Our praise should be for what we know He is going to do. Our thanks should be for what God is getting ready to bring us into.

God's Faith Building Process

We need to thank Him and give Him glory in advance of His deliverance as we learn and grow though His Faith Building Process. Our ability to say, "God, I thank You in advance" is just as real a Faith gesture as it is to say, "God, I trust Your Word and I'm going for it."

It starts with the dream – we read the Word, we believe the Word.

Then, we have to make a decision. Are we going to believe the Word and do it? Are we going to build on the Word and step out in faith?

Then, we will experience delay. "Though the vision tarry, wait for it. Thought it lingers, it is surely going to come to pass."

Then, there will be difficulty – circumstances and critics will come and you will come to what appears to be a dead end.

But, even though you don't know what else to do – it is a set up for God's deliverance, the final step in God's Faith Building Process.

BELIEVE

Reflection

Describe the connection between faith and works/deeds (corresponding acts of obedience). Can you have one without the other?

What dream has God given you? Have you decided how you will invest? Have you determined what you will need to let go of to move forward?

Think of a time you experienced delay and difficulty, how did God help you as you went through it?

How do you handle the dead ends?

What are you expecting God to do in your life?

Chapter 8
The Fight of Faith for Your Future

When Ahaz son of Jotham, the son of Uzziah, was king of Judah, King Rezin of Aram and Pekah son of Remaliah king of Israel marched up to fight against Jerusalem, but they could not overpower it. Now the house of David was told, "Aram has allied itself with Ephraim"; so the hearts of Ahaz and his people were shaken, as the trees of the forest are shaken by the wind. Then the Lord said to Isaiah, "Go out, you and your son Shear-Jashub, to meet Ahaz at the end of the aqueduct of the Upper Pool, on the road to the Launderer's Field. Say to him, 'Be careful, keep calm and don't be afraid. Do not lose heart because of these two smoldering stubs of firewood—because of the fierce anger of Rezin and Aram and of the son of Remaliah. Aram, Ephraim and Remaliah's son have plotted your ruin, saying,

BELIEVE

"Let us invade Judah; let us tear it apart and divide it among ourselves, and make the son of Tabeel king over it." Yet this is what the Sovereign Lord says: "'It will not take place, it will not happen, for the head of Aram is Damascus, and the head of Damascus is only Rezin. Within sixty-five years Ephraim will be too shattered to be a people. The head of Ephraim is Samaria, and the head of Samaria is only Remaliah's son. If you do not stand firm in your faith, you will not stand at all."'
~Isaiah 7:1-9

As we begin our final chapter in the discovery of real Biblical faith and its significance, my prayer is that you will never conclude your decision to live by faith. Why is this so crucial? The enemy is on a mission to steal our faith. We need to be practical and pragmatic as we fight in faith for our future.

The Fight of Faith for Your Future

In Isaiah 7:1-9, we read about the situation in which Ahaz finds himself,

> *When Ahaz son of Jotham, the son of Uzziah, was king of Judah, King Rezin of Aram and Pekah son of Remaliah king of Israel marched up to fight against Jerusalem, but they could not overpower it. Now the house of David was told, "Aram has allied itself with Ephraim" so the hearts of Ahaz and his people were shaken, as the trees of the forest are shaken by the wind.*

> *Then the Lord said to Isaiah, "Go out, you and your son Shear-Jashub, to meet Ahaz at the end of the aqueduct of the Upper Pool, on the road to the Launderer's Field. Say to him, 'Be careful, keep calm and don't be afraid. Do not lose heart because of these two smoldering stubs of firewood—because of the fierce anger of Rezin and Aram and of the son of Remaliah. Aram, Ephraim and Remaliah's son have plotted your ruin, saying, "Let us invade Judah; let us tear it apart and divide it among ourselves, and make the son of Tabeel king over it."*

BELIEVE

*Yet this is what the Sovereign Lord says: "It will not take place, it will not happen, for the head of Aram is Damascus, and the head of Damascus is only Rezin. Within sixty-five years Ephraim will be too shattered to be a people. The head of Ephraim is Samaria, and the head of Samaria is only Remaliah's son. **If you do not stand firm in your faith, you will not stand at all.**"*

Throughout this book, we have been examining real Biblical faith and the important role it plays in our lives as believers.

We are living in interesting times, times in which many are making the choice to no longer believe God and His Word in regard to marriage, family, and the definition of life. In everyday life, it is evident in the prejudice against and marginalization of individuals that people are choosing to no longer believe God. As we have walked through the Word, we have been working to discover how to be true believers, living our lives with the foundation of real faith. Why?

The Fight of Faith for Your Future

Because much is said and done in the name of faith that is not real faith at all. We have worked to separate fact from fiction and get a true understanding according to the Word of God of what faith is and what it looks like to live it consistently every day.

We know from God's Word in Hebrews 11:6, *"And without faith it is impossible to please God, because anyone who comes to him must believe that he exists and that he rewards those who earnestly seek him."* Yes, it is a sobering scripture because when we really understand the significance and profundity of this verse then we understand that no matter what we accomplish in life, no matter the size of our bank account, no matter the number of degrees we earn, and no matter the number of our social media following – we can have all of those and still not please God.

We please God through faith. There is an obscure scripture which challenges us in this regard. It is in Romans 14:23 where Paul tells us just how important faith is when he says, *"Anything that is not done in faith is sin."*

BELIEVE

We have to be committed to live by faith. It is a daily decision we have to make in order to honor and please God. It is the reason the concluding chapter of this book is entitled "The Fight of Faith for Your Future." God wants us to be prepared for the fight that is to come.

What does that mean? It is incredibly important for us to understand that in the days and in the months and in the years to come the enemy will place hurdles and obstacles and issues in our paths designed to get us to abandon our faith. It is especially true when we make up our minds to live by faith and honor God by faith. The enemy will do whatever he can possibly do to steal our faith.

The enemy is not after our cars – he does not drive; he is not after our homes – he has a place to live. The enemy is not after the stuff we think he is after – he is after our faith. Why? He knows he cannot stop what God has for us but if he can get us to abandon our faith, if he can steal our faith, then he can remove the conduit through which the kingdom of God flows into our lives as believers.

The Fight of Faith for Your Future

Faith is the currency of the kingdom. We cannot connect with God or transact business with God apart from faith. It is the reason the enemy will do whatever he can do to steal our faith.

We find Ahaz in Isaiah 7 in a very unique predicament. There is an army which marches against Ahaz and initially they are unsuccessful. After their unsuccessful attempt to fight Ahaz, they go and ally themselves, aligning with the other enemies of Ahaz. With the new alliances, their army grows bigger and they become more formidable as they prepare again to march against Ahaz.

Ahaz finds out they are returning but they are not the same army they were in the earlier battle. Ahaz begins shaking in fear as trees shake in the wind. His fear triggers God to touch the prophet Isaiah and tell him to go to Ahaz and give Him this Word. God tells Ahaz, *"Don't worry about the army, what they are planning will not happen BUT you must stand firm in your faith."* He goes on, *"If you do not stand firm in your faith, you will not stand at all."* In order to be victorious, Ahaz must stand firm in his faith.

BELIEVE

Beyond this being a true Biblical story with all sorts of applications for our lives, it is also a picture of what we will go through in the fight of faith for our future. There will be situations which will come into our lives in the future and the enemy will use them in an attempt to make us so fearful, so afraid, that we end up abandoning our faith. When we face difficult circumstances or challenges, we have to make the decision to live by faith, remembering it is a journey not a single step. On every journey, even one in which we are doing the will of God, challenges, obstacles, and issues will come which we don't expect. They are sometimes put in our path by the enemy, designed to make us so afraid or so uncertain that we abandon our faith and try to take matters into our own hands instead of trusting God.

As we move forward, the Word of God for us is the same Word that God speaks through Isaiah to Ahaz, *"if you don't stand firm in your faith, you will not stand at all."* We will have some fights of faith in the future. What is interesting about this notion of our fight of faith is that the Apostle Paul talks about it – a lot!

The Fight of Faith for Your Future

In 1 Timothy 6:12, Paul warns Timothy, his son in the faith, who he had been mentoring for quite some time. Timothy had been with Paul through his first, second, and third missionary journeys. As we get to what we know as the books of 1 and 2 Timothy, Paul knows his time on earth is coming to an end and he is preparing Timothy for life after him. Timothy is a young man Paul has been grooming to be an effective leader in the body of Christ. In this passage, Paul tells Timothy, *"Fight the good fight of the faith. Take hold of the <u>eternal life</u> to which you were called when you made your good confession in the presence of many witnesses"* (1 Timothy 6:12).

The Bible teaches us, as believers, we are all engaged in spiritual warfare and in the New Testament, this is the only fight (the fight of faith) in which we are encouraged to engage. Paul tells Timothy we have to fight it, taking hold to our calling – eternal life. Eternal life here is not simply referring to our coming life in heaven with God.

BELIEVE

The phrase used for "eternal life" means "life more abundant." Paul is saying if we want to live the life that God wants for us, the abundant life, then we have to engage in the fight of faith. Paul knows, from experience, the enemy is going to try to do anything and everything he can to discourage, dissuade, and get us to abandon our faith so he can short circuit what God has for us.

The way Paul speaks of victory has everything to do with keeping the faith as he testifies in 2 Timothy 4:7, saying, *"I have fought the good fight, I have finished the race, I have kept the faith."*

The Bible offers us a clear picture of what it means to finish strong and achieve victory. Those who are called victorious and strong kept the faith until the end, and the same is true for us – finishing strong and achieving victory requires us to keep the faith until the very end.

Our definition of success is very different than God's definition of success. Often success for us has a "destination" or "goal" attached – like a winning season, a well-paying job, a house in a desirable neighborhood, a particular standard of living.

God's definition is different. For God, success is who we are becoming along our journey. For God, success answers the questions, "Were you mature enough to believe Me even to the very end? Did you trust Me not only in the good times but in the bad times?" If we can demonstrate that we trust God with everything – we look more and more like Jesus who trusted the Father even to the very end. This is exactly what God desires for us! Paul had been shipwrecked, beaten, attacked, wrongly accused, imprisoned, but at every stage he fought the fight and kept the faith.

The writer of Hebrews in chapter 10, verses 38-39, explains, "*'But my righteous one will live by faith. And I take no pleasure in the one who shrinks back.' But we do not belong to those who shrink back and are destroyed, but to those who have faith and are saved.*" The one who "shrinks back" is the one who falls away but the ones who are saved are those who have faith. As believers, we lean in because we know God will deliver. We know faith in God always pays off! God is reminding us that there will be days, challenges, and moments where we don't know what to do – but if we don't stand firm in our faith we won't stand at all.

BELIEVE

The Bible spends a lot of time giving accolades and kudos to people of faith who endure to the end, people who hold onto their faith. Likewise, the Bible also speaks negatively about the people who have departed from the faith, abandoned their faith, and shipwrecked their faith.

Interestingly when the Bible references people who have shipwrecked their faith or abandoned their faith it is always connected to something the enemy convinced them to do.

In 1 Timothy 1:18-20 (NLT), Paul writes:

> *Timothy, my son, here are my instructions for you, based on the prophetic words spoken about you earlier. May they help you fight well in the Lord's battles. <u>Cling to your faith</u> in Christ, and keep your conscience clear. For some people have deliberately violated their consciences; as a result, <u>their faith has been shipwrecked</u>. Hymenaeus and Alexander are two examples. I threw them out and handed them over to Satan so they might learn not to blaspheme God."*

The Fight of Faith for Your Future

Hymenaeus and Alexander were two people in the church that Paul and Timothy knew well. Apparently Satan had something to do with these two individuals abandoning their faith. Paul used it as an example of what not to do.

In 1 Timothy 4:1-2, Paul says, *"The Spirit clearly says that in later times some will <u>abandon the faith</u> and follow deceiving spirits and things taught by demons. Such teachings come through hypocritical liars, whose consciences have been seared as with a hot iron."* He explains some people abandon the faith because they follow deceiving spirits and things taught by demons. There is a connection between Satan and demonic activity and people abandoning their faith.

Paul goes on in 1 Timothy 6:20-21 (NLT), *"Timothy, guard what God has entrusted to you. Avoid godless, foolish discussions with those who oppose you with their so-called knowledge. Some people have <u>wandered from the faith</u> by following such foolishness."*

BELIEVE

Paul says there is another group of people who follow foolishness and as a result they have wandered from the faith. Paul says we must avoid foolish discussions because they are ultimately a waste of time. Satan will use people, situations, and issues to try to get us to abandon our faith.

Jesus speaks of it in the Parable of the Sower in Mark 4:14-20 (TPT):

Let me explain: The farmer sows the message of the kingdom. What falls on the beaten path represents those who hear the message, but immediately Satan appears and snatches it from their hearts. And what is sown on gravel represents those who hear the message and receive it joyfully, but because their hearts fail to sink a deep root, they don't endure for long. For when trouble or persecution comes on account of the message, they immediately wilt and fall away. And what is sown among thorns represents those who hear the message, but they allow the cares of this life and the seduction of wealth and the desires for other things to crowd out and choke the message so that it produces nothing.

The Fight of Faith for Your Future

But what is sown on good soil represents those who open their hearts to receive the message and their lives bear good fruit—some yield a harvest of thirty, sixty, even a hundredfold!"

The enemy works in a number of ways to get us to abandon our faith. As soon as we get a Word of faith, immediately Satan seeks to snatch it away from our hearts. He does not want God's Word to be rooted in our hearts because when it is our lives are changed! When trouble and persecution come, if God's Word is only in our heads and not rooted in our hearts, we fall away. At other times, we hear the Word and believe it, but we aren't truly rooted in it, so Satan uses all the other things in our lives to distract us so the Word does not produce positive change in our lives.

We need to be prepared for battle because the enemy will do what he can to get us to abandon the faith. When we proclaim we are going to live by faith for God, the enemy immediately says, "Let's see…" as he hurls challenges, issues, and obstacles at us. Let's look at some practical ways we can recognize Satan's efforts to steal our faith.

BELIEVE

What Will Steal Your Faith?
(What Will The Enemy Use To Steal Your Faith?)

<u>Adverse Circumstances</u>

The first thing the enemy loves to use against us is adverse circumstances – problematic challenges. One of the greatest example of this is in Matthew 14:28-31, when Peter walks on the water. Matthew writes,

"'Lord, if it's you,' Peter replied, 'tell me to come to you on the water.'

Come,' he said. Then Peter got down out of the boat, walked on the water and came toward Jesus.

But when he saw the wind, he was afraid and, beginning to sink, cried out, 'Lord, save me!'

Immediately Jesus reached out his hand and caught him. 'You of little faith,' he said, 'why did you doubt?'

We know that *"Faith comes by hearing and hearing by the Word of God."* What prompted Peter to get out of the boat? The Word of God – Jesus told him to *"Come."* Peter gets out and walking on water heads toward Jesus.

When he starts looking at the wind and the waves, he begins to sink, but even without the wind or the waves, he would not be able to walk on water. He could walk on the water only because of His faith in the Word of God.

When we come against adverse circumstances we must remember the wind and the waves do not deter what God said. Often we are in a situation in which God spoke it, we believed it, so we follow but then we abandon our faith in the situation because of adverse conditions. The adverse conditions don't change or nullify the Word of God – God is looking for people who will stand on His Word no matter what!

Distractions

In addition to adverse circumstances, the enemy will try to use distractions to steal your faith. Distractions are those things which we allow to become idols in our lives like "the seduction of wealth and desires for things." An idol is any person, place, or thing that we love more than the Lord. We have all faced them on our faith journeys, myself included.

BELIEVE

When we find ourselves in that place, if we can acknowledge there are some potential distractions in our lives, we can firm up our defenses so the enemy cannot use those distractions against us. If we fail to do so, we may end up loving our "idols" more and ultimately abandoning our faith.

In Mark 14:3-11, Jesus explains how money can be a distraction for us as it was for Judas:

> *While he was in Bethany, reclining at the table in the home of Simon the Leper, a woman came with an alabaster jar of very expensive perfume, made of pure nard. She broke the jar and poured the perfume on his head.*

> *Some of those present were saying indignantly to one another, 'Why this waste of perfume? It could have been sold for more than a year's wages and the money given to the poor.' And they rebuked her harshly.*

The Fight of Faith for Your Future

'Leave her alone,' said Jesus. 'Why are you bothering her? She has done a beautiful thing to me. The poor you will always have with you, and you can help them any time you want. But you will not always have me. She did what she could. She poured perfume on my body beforehand to prepare for my burial. Truly I tell you, wherever the gospel is preached throughout the world, what she has done will also be told, in memory of her.'

Then Judas Iscariot, one of the Twelve, went to the chief priests to betray Jesus to them. They were delighted to hear this and promised to give him money. So he watched for an opportunity to hand him over."

The woman had taken the equivalent value of a year's salary and gave it to Jesus and they rebuked her. But Jesus praised her. Then Judas – the accountant of Jesus's ministry, was upset. Why? While he loved the Lord, he loved money more. Money had become his idol and when he saw the waste in her actions and Jesus's praise, he decided to put a stop to the ministry.

BELIEVE

If we have distractions – that which we love more than the Lord – those distractions are exactly what the enemy will use to enter our life and get us to abandon our faith.

Do you have something else or someone else that you love more than Jesus? Part of the reason, He said give it all to Me is because if you are really going to live by faith, He has to be number one in your life – there can be no Plan B. If you are truly going to trust Him, you are going to have to let go of all the other "stuff." Here is the blessing – when you give it all to Him – He promises to take care of everything!

Words Of Unbelief

The enemy uses adverse circumstances and distractions but he also uses words of unbelief. I have had the honor of sharing the gospel of Jesus around the world. There was a pastor in China whose wife was diagnosed with cancer. The doctors gave her six months, but three years into her cancer battle she was still alive and she and her husband were standing on the Word of God.

As someone who is been privileged to preach the Word around the world, I often advise international believers that there are some things we simply don't need to bring over from America because some believers who live in different countries believe the American church is the pinnacle.

An American Missionary came to the town of the Pastor in China and was invited to his house to pray for his wife. The American Missionary was from a denomination which did not really believe that Jesus could heal people, but he came and prayed a weak prayer. As he finished praying and was leaving their house, he saw on their wall a verse of scripture written in their native language. The American Missionary pointed to it and asked, "What is that?"

The pastor said, "That is Isaiah 53:5, *'By His stripes, we are healed.'*"

The American Missionary said, "That's good, but you do know that is about eternity, it does not mean God heals in real life."

BELIEVE

One month later, the pastor's wife died. She had been fighting cancer for three years while standing on the Word of God. They invited someone who came in with words of unbelief, and shortly after that encounter, she died, because words can kill.

Matthew 5:22 (MSG) says *"… The simple moral fact is that words kill."* Sometimes having the wrong people around us will destroy our faith.

When we got ready to buy our first building, we were less than a year old as a church. We were renting a Seventh Day Adventist Church and we had outgrown it. The economy was headed down, a precursor to the 2008 crash, and we thought there was no way we could build from the ground up. We were believing God for a building, exercising our faith, though the banks were saying it couldn't happen. When we stepped foot on the property of the first building we purchased, the Holy Spirit said to me, "This is the place!"

We had meetings. We prayed, in fact I called one of my pastor friends who had been influential in my life for years and asked him to pray. I explained how God had spoken to me and that we were planning to buy the building for $2.5M. He said, "Man, are you crazy? That is foolish. It is not wisdom. It is not good stewardship. The church is only a year old and you are about to lead them into that kind of debt. No bank is going to lend you the money and if they do it will be the worst decision you ever make."

I was shocked because for so much of my life I had looked to him for words of encouragement and support. I was uneasy because I was torn between what I knew God had said and the words of unbelief coming from my friend. My struggle was more difficult than it needed to be. I never told him how his words impacted me until The People Factor book was released and I had to get him to sign off on the story being included in the book. I told him how his response made me feel because in that moment I needed someone to believe God with me and he provided only words of unbelief.

BELIEVE

We had meetings. We prayed, in fact I called one of
my pastor friends who had been influential in my life
for years and asked him to pray. I explained how God
had spoken to me and that we were planning to buy the
building for $2.5M. He said, "Man, are you crazy? That is
foolish. It is not wisdom. It is not good stewardship. The
church is only a year old and you are about to lead them
into that kind of debt. No bank is going to lend you the
money and if they do it will be the worst decision you
ever make."

I was shocked because for so much of my life I had
looked to him for words of encouragement and support.
I was uneasy because I was torn between what I knew
God had said and the words of unbelief coming from
my friend. My struggle was more difficult than it needed
to be. I never told him how his words impacted me until
The People Factor book was released and I had to get
him to sign off on the story being included in the book.
I told him how his response made me feel because in
that moment I needed someone to believe God with me
and he provided only words of unbelief.

The Fight of Faith for Your Future

There will be lots of time when we get into the Word and find guidance but in those times we have to shut out words of unbelief from others in our lives. It doesn't mean they are bad people but we have to realize we are on a journey of faith that they are not on – it doesn't mean we need to dump them as friends but we might need to redefine the parameters of our friendship to avoid their words of unbelief. We need to establish friendships which encourage us to believe God.

Jesus modeled this truth when He went to Jairus's house to perform a miracle. By the time He got there everyone was wailing. Jesus arrived and said, *"She is not dead, she's asleep"* and then He put all the wailers outside the house. He didn't want those who did not believe in the house.

The enemy will use people and things to trip us up in our faith journey and we need to learn how to put them out of our house! There are people we need around us and people we do NOT need around us. We don't need to be surrounded by people who are not on a faith journey, who don't have the faith to believe God with us!

BELIEVE

Bad Theology or Tradition

The enemy also uses bad theology or tradition to steal our faith. The pastor who spoke words of unbelief to me was not a bad guy, but he is of a tradition that historically hasn't leaned into a life of faith. There are things God has done in my life that he will never see as a result because he is of a faith tradition that is dry and traditional, and makes no space for God to move through faith. Jesus describes it in Mark 7:13, *"Thus you nullify the word of God by your tradition that you have handed down. And you do many things like that."*

You cannot base your faith on the experiences of other people. You simply cannot because people will say, "That can never be done." Why? They are saying what they believe is possible from their own experience. It is the reason I had to change the dynamic of the friendship I mentioned earlier. God did provide the building and what we needed to sustain the ministry. It was not that God could not do it, but my friend's words were based on his bad theology and tradition. To him, a church only a year old buying a $2.5M building was unheard of!

The Fight of Faith for Your Future

We cannot allow people who cannot believe God to come into the lane of the race we are called to run. In Hebrews 12:1, we read, *"Therefore, since we are surrounded by such a great cloud of witnesses, let us throw off everything that hinders and the sin that so easily entangles. And let us run with perseverance the race marked out for us."* When I ran track in high school, we had the fastest team. Even so there were times we were disqualified because we crossed over into someone else's lane. God's Word says there is a race marked out for us to run and we need to run our race. In other words, "Stay in your lane." Stop trying to bring the experiences of other people, which don't line up with the Word of God to you, into your lane. If God says, "Do it" then stand on the Word and stay in your lane.

If someone has a testimony of the goodness and faithfulness of God because they have trusted the Word and stood on the Word, then bring them into your lane! But if someone is telling you all the ways it can't be done, you need to proclaim, "I believe God" and tell them to stay in their lane while you run the race marked out for you!

BELIEVE

Imposters

The enemy will try to use imposters to steal your faith. This is a very sobering topic, but let's reread 1 Timothy 4:1-2 which says, "The Spirit clearly says that in later times some will abandon the faith and follow deceiving spirits and things taught by demons. Such teachings come through hypocritical liars, whose consciences have been seared as with a hot iron." Deceiving spirits are the work of the enemy. The Bible tells us Satan masquerades as an angel of light and also that he is the prince of this world. There are many things in the world today that are the tricks and tools of the enemy, each designed to lead us astray. Paul is telling us there are imposters, people who will look one way and seem to be believers. They will infiltrate the church and our lives with the express purpose to lead us astray.

In Jude 1:3-4, we read:
Dear friends, although I was very eager to write to you about the salvation we share, I felt compelled to write and urge you to contend for the faith that was once for all entrusted to God's holy people.

The Fight of Faith for Your Future

For certain individuals whose condemnation was written about long ago have secretly slipped in among you. They are ungodly people, who pervert the grace of our God into a license for immorality and deny Jesus Christ our only Sovereign and Lord.

Jude says the imposters slip in and pervert the grace of God. The imposters will say, "That's not a big deal, God knows your heart."

We live in a world right now where there is much happening in the name of Christ but is NOT Christ at all! Believers are buying into it and falling for it, rather than taking the time to ensure it lines up with the Word of God. The enemy uses imposters and there are believers who have abandoned their faith because of those imposters. We need to get in the Word and know the difference!

BELIEVE

In Matthew 7:15-20, 21-23 (MSG), Jesus warns us:

*Be wary of false preachers who smile a lot, dripping with practiced sincerity. Chances are they are out to rip you off some way or other. Don't be impressed with charisma; **look for character.** Who preachers are is the main thing, not what they say. A genuine leader will never exploit your emotions or your pocketbook. These diseased trees with their bad apples are going to be chopped down and burned...*

'Knowing the correct password—saying 'Master, Master,' for instance—isn't going to get you anywhere with me. What is required is serious obedience—doing what my Father wills. I can see it now—at the Final Judgment thousands strutting up to me and saying, 'Master, we preached the Message, we bashed the demons, our super-spiritual projects had everyone talking.' And do you know what I am going to say? 'You missed the boat. All you did was use me to make yourselves important. You don't impress me one bit. You're out of here.'

He is saying loud and clear, "Just because it is popular doesn't mean it is God."

The Fight of Faith for Your Future

In Acts 17, the Christians at Berea were more noble than the Thessalonians because they examined the scriptures to see if what Paul was saying is true. We are called to do the same. We cannot simply like, and post, and repost what is popular – we have to get in the Word for ourselves and make sure what is being said is lining up with the Word of God. We have to study the Word for ourselves because it is the only way to tell if someone is real or faking it.

In 2 Thessalonians 2:9-10, Paul warns us, *"The coming of the lawless one will be in accordance with how Satan works. He will use all sorts of displays of power through signs and wonders that serve the lie, and all the ways that wickedness deceives those who are perishing. They perish because they <u>refused to love the truth</u> and so be saved."*

BELIEVE

It does not say they did not have the Truth, but that they did not love it. If we are going to honor God with our faith, if we are going to live by faith, if we are going to stand on His Word, we have to love the Truth more than anything else.

Reflection

We've talked a lot about the power of God in this book. Think about what you have learned and a time you experienced the power of God and share it with someone close to you.

In scripture, we see God's people witness the power of God's Word but still not believe.
The Word is so powerful, but unbelief is also powerful. Give an example of the power of unbelief in your life (this may be easier than giving an example of the power of faith in your life because we are so bombarded by doubt/fear from the world's perspective - remember we are in a fight!)

How did the power of God's Word help you overcome your fear and fight for your future?

What has you worried right now? How can you honor God, live by faith, stand on His Word, and trust Him for your future in your current situation?

ON THIS PODCAST, WE EXPLORE A VARIETY OF TOPICS THAT ARE CRITICAL TO A LIFE OF FREEDOM, PURPOSE, AND FULFILLMENT.

SUBSCRIBE NOW!

FOR INFO ABOUT BOOKS,
READING PLANS, LEADERSHIP &
DISCIPLESHIP RESOURCES ,
AND SO MUCH MORE VISIT
VANMOODY.ORG

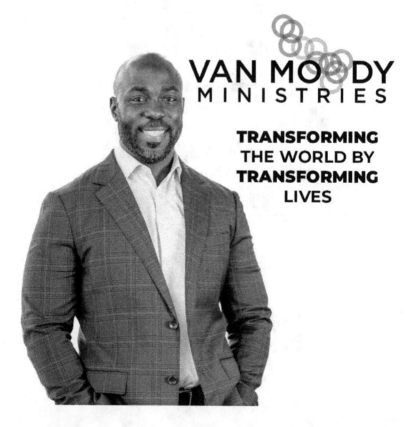

VAN MOODY
MINISTRIES

TRANSFORMING
THE WORLD BY
TRANSFORMING
LIVES